Pioneer Marriage

J. Frank McGowan

Dedication

This book is dedicated to the brave pioneers that forged their way from the midwest to the western part of our great country. These brave and hardy people were made of truly great stock. The tremendous fortitude that they had to have to accomplish this task is unbelievable to us.

We, the benefactors of their efforts, will be forever grateful and in awe of their effort.

John F. ' Frank' McGowan

Foreward

The McGowan family has always been quite proud of its heritage. The children were always reminded by our elders, "Your Wilson great-grandparents were the first white family to live in Mason Valley", and "your great-grandmother was the first white woman to live in Mason Valley". As young children we just shrugged off these declarations from these elders. But as time evolved and we grew older, we wrote essays at school of our pioneer ancestors and stories of the family's well-known individuals. Old photographs were exchanged. Paintings and charcoal drawings by family artists were occasionally brought forth of our older ancestors.

As we aged, there were family members who had made " family trees" of our heritage that we all enjoyed. History books about Nevada and its first inhabitants were brought to our attention. People would occasionally ask questions of us that involved our families Scottish and Irish backgrounds.

Our aunt, Kathryn McGowan Buchanan, built a very large family photo album that garnered considerable attention of both family members and many others. 'Katie' became more and more popular as the years rolled by and she became the family matriarch and historian. She started a luncheon of interested family females to display and discuss her collection of family history and photos at length with her. This became a very popular event.

Then, on April 21, 2021, at the age of 99, Kate passed away. Her death was a tremendous loss to her family and multitude of friends. Our beloved family matriarch and historian was gone. She left a superb amount of McGowan and Wilson memorabilia of historical photos and history.

The most interesting and precious history of the McGowan and Wilsons had to be preserved. Within the family there needed to be a place created to save this wonderful history for future generations to enable them to see how we are joined together.

Katie's death left me in the position of McGowan family patriarch. While being forever grateful for life as a McGowan, I'm not sure that the job of family historian and patriarch is in the best hands. The rich history of the families has always intrigued me and interest in it has been an endeavor over the years of my retirement. This book is the result of many of our family members contributions of photos, stories, histories, family trees and many, many conversations. I have used history books, newspaper articles and photos, encyclopedias, historical organizations, libraries, and stories acquired in numerous places, in addition to our own books and family gathered material. I will touch later on the people who assisted me in "Contributions".

One of the great tasks with this work has been to be correct with names, relationships, dates, and events in our history. While erring is inevitable, we hope to capture as much as possible correctly, to help future generations understand the who, what, where, when and why of our family story. So......we plunge in! Hoping to tell as accurately as possible the story of how we all became related.

Acknowledgements

The gathering of family history began many years ago with Katherine 'Katie' McGowan Buchanan the only daughter of the two principles of Pioneer Marriage. Her stories, both written and oral. and her family photo album were the beginning of the collection which continues to this day.

Darrell McGowan, my son, has taught me how to author and create a book. He is really the literary engineer that has allowed me to tell the McGowan and Wilson family stories and show the photos of everyone. Also, he is the author of two very good books.

The family genealogist through this endeavor was my third cousin once removed, Judy Ellis from Payson Arizona. Her grandmother, Beth Wilson Ellis . was a playmate of her aunt. Elizabeth 'Beth' Wilson. She's a California retired teacher who was an immense help finding lost relatives.

A number of the quotes are those of Earl William Kersten Sr., a past professor at the University of Nevada and Reno resident. The information came, with permission from his son Earl Jr. from his father's PH.D. dissertation, "SETTLEMENTS AND ECONOMIC LIFE IN THE WALKER RIVER COUNTRY OF NEVADA AND CALIFORNIA".

Daughters Mary McGowan Bright and Ann McGowan Bray have unselfishly helped as literary and graphic creators and editors from the beginning to the end of this book.

Cousins Kathy Buchanan McClintock and Kim Perkins Miller have helped secure needed information, photos, and other data crucial to this endeavor.

Daughter- in- law Susan McGowan created the very nice layout for the front page.

This book relied on a number of written documents to substantiate and/or verify family historical knowledge, among which were:
Thompson & West History of Nevada 1861
Wikipedia
"Mason Valley News"
"Yerington Times"
"Nevada State Journal"
Wovoka and the Ghost Dance by Michael Hickman
The Valley of the Walker Rivers by Phyllis Matheus

Contents

Dedication

Forward

Acknowledgements

David and Abigail Head West

The California Gold Rush of 1948-49 created a great western migration in the United States. People from all over the the world had heard the news of the gold in the foothills of what is now California and they were in a hurry to stake their claim and become rich.

This is about two families and their journeys and the exciting lives and families that followed that great land rush.

This part of the story (much of which was supplied by our family genealogist, Judy Ellis of Payson, Arizona) is about two David Wilsons; the father, David Wilson, and his son, also named David Wilson. The father was born in 1798 in Pennsylvania to descendants of Scotch-Irish immigrants who had lived there since the mid 1700's. He moved to Harrison County, Ohio as a young man to continue farming in the family tradition. He acquired farmland and married Elizabeth Ferrier on December 6, 1817. She is believed to have come from the same area of Pennsylvania. David married Nancy Kennedy after Elizabeth's death. David and Elizabeth had five daughters, Catherine, Elizabeth, Mary, Louisa, and Nancy and three sons, James, William and David. David's son, David, was born in 1829. When he was nine years old, his father, having received land grants in Missouri as a veteran of the War of 1812, moved the family to Scotland County, Missouri. It was here that David and his brothers James and William grew into manhood.

In 1850, the irresistible attraction of the California gold discoveries drew the three young brothers, James (26), William (24), and David (21). They traveled by boat down the Mississippi River and across the Gulf of Mexico to the Isthmus of Panama.

The oldest brother, James, contracted malaria while they were walking across the Isthmus of Panama and had to be left behind. David and William hurried on and boarded a boat and finished their journey to San Francisco. They then went on land to the Sierra Nevada Mountains and the Yuba River where they placer mined for gold.

Three years later in 1853, David received word that his father was gravely ill. He left his brother William and the gold mining and returned to Missouri. This time he took a ship around the Cape of Hope, which took several months, to the Gulf of Mexico and up the Mississippi River to Missouri and finally home to attend to his father until his death (September 15, 1857) at age 79.

In 1855, David, age 26, married Abigail Jane Butler, age 19, in Missouri. Six years later, in 1861, after the start of the Civil War, David joined the Union Army. He took part in the battle of Athens under Col. Moore, but suffered sun stroke and was honorably discharged.

The eastern half of the United States was well populated and starting to become industrialized. The United States had already elected sixteen presidents. Abraham Lincoln was the current president. The western half of the country from the Mississippi River westward hadn't seen as much population growth. The far western states beyond the Rocky Mountains and Sierra Nevada Mountains were very sparsely inhabited. The Native Americans were by far the most populous group. There were very few roads and no railroads. It was still the western frontier. The American Indian Wars were still taking place.

David and Abigail in 1862 with four young children, Louisa W (8), James W (6), Joseph I (4), and George W (1), left Missouri for Iowa with everything they owned, and headed west by wagon train. It is believed they took The Mormon Trail where they would travel over 1,900 miles by wagon, horseback and on foot. They crossed plains, rivers, streams, mountains and deserts. Through the heat and cold, rain and wind, dust and mud, they took their young children, their livestock and their

provisions on the treacherous trip with about 50 other wagons in a very large group. The tiring ordeal would last four to five months from beginning to end, averaging 11-17 miles a day. Some wagons were forced to quit due to sickness, broken equipment or other hardships. The Mormon Trail took them through

parts of Iowa, Nebraska and Wyoming. In Wyoming they connected with the California Trail going through parts of Idaho,

Utah and into Nevada. The exact dates and routes the Wilsons took are not recorded. They possibly went as far north as the "City of Rocks" in Idaho or further south into Colorado. Somehow they found a way over the Rocky Mountains and finally entered Nevada Territory at about the present day Wells township. The trail then followed the Humboldt River to the Humboldt Sink south and west of the current Lovelock area. The next part of the journey was only a short distance but it was considered one of the most treacherous. It was known as the Forty Mile Desert. The Humboldt River is reduced to a muddy trickle and is the last source of potable water before a forty mile trek through dry alkali wasteland. It was the most disliked portion of the California Trail. Many of the immigrants and their livestock perished there in the dry and hot sandy desert. Some even traveled at night to escape the heat.

The Carson River's fresh water was the reward for making it through those treacherous forty miles. The family could then rest while David rendezvoused with his brother William, who had been working a claim with a partner near Virginia City. William encouraged David and family to go to Mason Valley where there was available land to claim and fine water for farming.

Another twenty miles and David Wilson and family of six were in Mason Valley for the first time from their arduous trip of near 2,000 miles from Missouri. They stopped in the South Western corner of the valley by the Walker River that would later be named Wilson Canyon. It was a beautiful sight to David and

Abigail as they started to make a makeshift home to begin their new life in the West.

Mason Valley in 1863 was a serene little valley in western Nevada not far from the very high Sierra Nevada Mountain Range. History tells us that along the river there were cottonwood trees and many willows and buck brush, along with other grassy vegetation. Sage and rabbit brush were nearby. There were patches of sloughs, with tules and native grasses, caused by the river flooding its banks through the centuries. This made a ideal place to

Wilson dug out home
Painting by John F Frank McGowan

5

start farming. There were no roads, bridges, stores or towns, only paths where previous travelers had passed through. History says the Wilsons were the first white family to live there. Abigail is considered the first white woman to settle in Mason Valley. The Mason Valley Times wrote, "There were only ranches in the valley when they arrived, Hock Mason, Charles Snyder and Angus McLeod, Tom & Joe Wheeler and a few more...."

Family stories told of a dug-out type shelter being constructed in the bank of the old river wash, using willows and tules for a roof to make a shelter that kept the family of six out of the weather. Tending to a one year-old baby along with three other children under ten years of age must have been a monumental task, especially without a house to live in.

Some of the history books of Nevada mention David Wilson of Mason Valley as one of the delegates to help frame the constitution of Nevada in 1863 as it was about to become a state. He didn't have a home to live in but he assisted the state in its need.

2

Wilson's New Home in Mason Valley

David had to fence an area for the livestock and start a new farm located in this uninhabited new place in the Utah Territory, which later became Mason Valley in Lyon County, Nevada. There were four ranches in the valley when they arrived. There was the Charles Snyder and Angus McLeod Ranch, the Hock Mason Ranch, the Billy Alcorn Ranch and the Tom and Joe Wheeler Ranch. This new country was quite different than Missouri, where they were from. It was much dryer here and quite primitive. This new land needed water brought to it. It could not be 'dry farmed' like Missouri.

To start his ranch, David purchased 230 acres from "Pap" Wheeler and his seven sons for $2,000. Water for irrigating was needed. A diversion dam in the river was created and ditches were dug to the fields he would farm. The task was very difficult in this primitive land of sage brush, buck brush and native grasses that grew near the river. David Wilson helped the Alcorn brothers cut hay with a scythe and put up

what was the first of many haystacks in the valley.

The 'Book of Nevada of 1861' stated, "For six months Abigail lived without seeing the face of another white woman, and we may imagine her joy when Mrs. Sprague, with her husband and daughter Alice, moved from Carson City. Mrs. Wilson, who was of a retiring nature, said, 'When I heard there was a woman in the next tent I did not wait to be introduced, but just put on my bonnet and went to see her, and how we talked!'"

David built the first ditch in the south end of the valley called the D&GW ditch (David and George Wilson ditch). According to 'The Mason Valley Times' of March 26, 1915, David Wilson started to build the Tunnel Ditch in 1872 and finished it in 1876. This was one of many ditches needed to irrigate their farm. From a small beginning, the Wilson properties grew to many hundreds of acres over the next few generations. It eventually included properties from the ranch by Wilson Canyon to a home and farm at Nordyke. David's three sons made quite a reputation as farmers and businessmen as they grew older and developed additional farming fields, ditches, and corrals for their livestock.

After the completion of the Union Pacific and Central Pacific intercontinental Railroad in 1869, David returned to Missouri to purchase 150 head of thoroughbred Durham cattle for the first dairy herd in Nevada. While David was establishing himself as a farmer and cattleman, Nevada was attempting to gain statehood, a process in which he became an active participant, helping frame a state constitution.

The Wilsons were staunch Republicans and Mason Valley Methodist Church members.

Thompson and West wrote in the 1881 History of Nevada, "Usually the Indians were friendly, but at one time, for some reason unknown, they put on their war-paint and executed a war-dance. Seven painted warriors camped opposite Mr. Wilson's house. He armed the six white men who lived with him, and they in turn stood guard several days and nights. All other white people in this valley fled to Fort Churchill, taking with them Mrs. Wilson's daughter who was visiting the Sprague family. No shots were fired and the Indians peacefully withdrew to their camps."

David Wilson never took his family away from the farm on these occasions. In the beginning years it was estimated there were near 2,000 Paiute Indians and 13 white families. A number of Paiute families worked for the Wilsons and were befriended by them. A son of a Paiute family became close friends with David Wilson's sons and later he became well-known nationally. His story will be told later.

David's wife, Abigail or 'Aunt Abbey Jane', as she was fondly called by her many friends and relatives, was a very busy and industrious woman, with a toddler and three other young children to help. In the beginning, a new home needed to be started along with feeding everyone, including farm hands. Stories from her family tell of her ingenuity in making soap from ashes, candles for lighting with beeswax, jelly from wild buck-berries, pillows from tule cattails, and doctoring the sick for their family and friends. She was a native of Ohio from a family 8 children.

Abigail & David Wilson

The Butler Family

Abigail Jane was the oldest and she had three brothers and five sisters. Her sisters, Sarah Elizabeth Butler, married Ulrich Strosnider, the founder of the Pitchfork Ranch; Hester Butler, married Hamilton Wise; Marry Elizabeth 'Molly' Butler, married Paul Strosnider; Rebecca Ann 'Becky' Butler married Aron Dunn. All married and migrated to Mason Valley except for Elizabeth 'Betty' Morris. One of her brothers, Isaac J. Butler, Jr. also migrated to Mason Valley. Abigail's two other brothers were Joseph and George Washington. (*Butler data was provided by Evan Pellegrini.*)

BUTLER SISTERS WITH MARRIED NAMES

During the 1860's, there were mining camps starting in the surrounding area that required meat, flour, and table food for their workers. This provided a very close and rich market for the Mason Valley ranchers. The mines also increased demand for hay to feed

the livestock that provided the transportation to all the camps. This helped to create a high price for hay and most farm products while the camps were running, but it also depressed the market prices when the ore ran out and they closed. Most mining operations had a short life.

Earl William Kersten, Jr. stated in his dissertation, SETTLEMENTS AND ECONOMIC LIFE IN THE WALKER RIVER COUNTRY OF NEVADA AND CALIFORNIA, *"In the decade of Aurora's greatness, 1860-69, extensive areas in Mason, Smith, East Walker, Sweetwater and Antelope valleys were settled by men primarily interested in stock-raising. The ranches were localized on the good lands of north central and south central Mason Valley and along West Walker River in south central Smith Valley, lands along the length of East Walker Valley from Mason Valley and in north central Antelope Valley. The agriculturalists obtained their lands largely by preemptions. Lacking government surveys, they made their*

own crude surveys and marked their lands with monuments. They filed their claims to these lands in Carson City, territorial capital before 1864, and state capital afterward."

The news of Mason Valley quickly spread and immigrants began to fill the valley with ranches and farms. In the middle of the valley a man named Geiger started a little general store. Roads, as primitive as they were, began to appear to most places of travel. Homes for the inhabitants were becoming visible. The Walker River, from the nearby Sierra Nevada Mountains, entered the valley from the canyon at the south west corner. From there it meandered across and down to the north east end of the valley, providing water that was needed to keep the valley beautifully green in the Nevada desert.

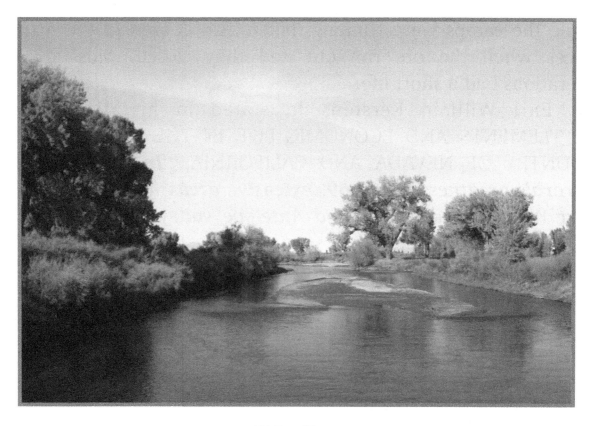

Walker River

3

Pine Grove Gold Discovery

David Wilson's older brother, William, joined David farming in Mason Valley. William still had a high interest in gold mining from over 10 years of previous experience in California and the Virginia City area. He maintained that interest while farming their new properties in Mason Valley.

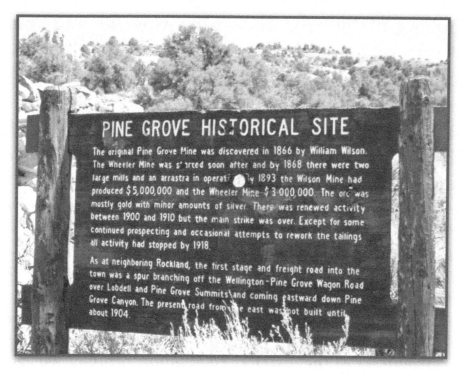

PINE GROVE HISTORICAL SITE

The original Pine Grove Mine was discovered in 1866 by William Wilson. The Wheeler Mine was started soon after and by 1868 there were two large mills and an arrastra in operation. By 1893 the Wilson Mine had produced $5,000,000 and the Wheeler Mine $3,000,000. The ore was mostly gold with minor amounts of silver. There was renewed activity between 1900 and 1910 but the main strike was over. Except for some continued prospecting and occasional attempts to rework the tailings all activity had stopped by 1918.

As at neighboring Rockland, the first stage and freight road into the town was a spur branching off the Wellington - Pine Grove Wagon Road over Lobdell and Pine Grove Summits and coming eastward down Pine Grove Canyon. The present road from the east was not built until about 1904.

There are a number of versions of this story that have been told. They are all quite similar. A Native American Paiute man who worked for the Wilsons, upon seeing a rock with gold in it said he knew where there were many of the same rocks and he explained

WILSON HOME 2 girls right Beth Ellis & Amy Wilson Brown

where. William Wilson explored the place that was described and discovered gold July 09, 1866. He filed a claim and David and he were partners in a mine that would produce between five and six million dollars of bullion. The strike was on and immediately droves of miners arrived in search of riches. William and David's claim was about 18 miles from the Wilson ranch.

In his dissertation, SETTLEMENTS AND ECONOMIC LIFE OF THE WALKER RIVER COUNTRY OF NEVADA AND CALIFORNIA, Earl William Kersten, Jr. wrote, *"The Esmeralda Union of Aurora reported August 11, 1866 that a stampede was in progress to this new discovery. The camp which grew up here was first named Wilsonville, but in a year or two, the name of Pine Grove became established. The sizable stands of piñon in the the vicinity inspired the name, it is said. A letter to the Mariposa Gazette in November, 1866 reported great activity at Wilsonville - William Wilson's discovery claim on the Himalaya ledge and the Wheeler brothers claim called the Mastodon were the centers of interest. From these claims developed the Wilson and Wheeler mines, the only major producers of the district. Their main product was gold.*

Pine Grove straggling for a mile up and down a narrow mountain canyon at an elevation near 7,000 feet, grew rapidly to reach a population of 600 by 1870, according to census population schedules. Water for the settlement came from nearby springs and from wells. The ore from the mines was processed by three mills powered by steam and

PINE GROVE

burning piñon wood. Three hotels, five saloons, variety store, hardware store, general store, dance hall and numerous shops provided for goods and services. The post office established here in 1868 at the height the boom suffered a decline of activity in the dying years of the camp after 1880, but it lingered here till after the turn of the century.

Pine Grove for several years served as the chief service center for Mason Valley and other low lands near by, though the town's position up in its mountain canyon was peripheral to this trading area. Ranchers from Mason, East Walker, and Smith valleys often came here for shopping and recreation. Mason Valley, the chief community, was very small and offered few services before 1875. Some Mason Valley ranchers had important interest in Pine Grove. The Wilson brothers were owners of a mine and mill, and S.D. (Charlie) Lane had a freight line. By the late 1870's Pine Grove had begun to slow down. Small-scale mining operations have been performed on several occasions since the major mining halted. In all, Pine Grove is estimated to have produced $5,000,000 worth of bullion."

PINE GROVE PAINTING by J. F. McGowan

Although the Wilson Mine produced a great amount of wealth, it has been pointed out that David and

William Wilson operated under the "Tribute System" through which many poor men secured small fortunes, although, they themselves, did not amass great fortunes. The price of gold in those days was only about $15.50 a Troy ounce. Todays 2024 market of $5 million bullion in the 1800's is over $2,000 per ounce would be $650,000,000!

It was fortunate that the Pine Grove area did not suffer a major fire during all of its years of operation. During that time, the little town had its share of excitement, including fights,

WILSIN MINE

WINTER AT PINE GROVE

brawls and shootings. The little cemetery, which still exists today, is

REMNANTS OF 5 STAMP MILL

on a hill north of the Wilson Mine. The small little schoolhouse still exists.

PAINTING MIMI JOBE

PINE GROVE SCHOOL

One of the most exciting occasions for the Wilsons happened in 1881. David and Abigail, at age 45, gave birth to their daughter, Elizabeth 'Beth' Jane, born January 26, 1881, seventeen years after her youngest brothers. She was the pride and joy of the whole family. She would grow up and attend school in Pine Grove.

The niece of Elizabeth Wilson, Beth Louise Ellis, although 10 years younger, was one one of the few female playmates available, lived up the mountain at the Rockland Mine. To play with each other it was necessary to walk the distance back and forth, which Beth Wilson enjoyed and did on numerous occasions.

Elizabeth Wilson's daughter, Katherine

BETH ELLIS

17

"Katie" Buchanan, liked to tell this story of her mother: "Elizabeth played with gold pieces as toys were so scarce. David Wilson would have his wife Abagail, with baby Elizabeth, haul the gold ore from Pine Grove to the mint in Carson City, Nevada in a buck wagon. He assumed this method was safe from robbery because no one would molest a woman and her young child."

In 1875, David Wilson and his sons purchased the entire interest of his brother and partner William and formed a copartnership, called David Wilson and Sons. On February 15, 1897, David sold his remaining interest in the partnership to his sons. Then in 1902, the Wilson mine sold to developers for $50,000. At this time the David Wilson family, after 25 years in Pine Grove, returned to Mason Valley to live.

PINE GROVE - WILSON HOTEL

WILSON HOTEL REMAINS - PINE GROVE
Painting by John F. 'Frank' McGowan - Artist

18

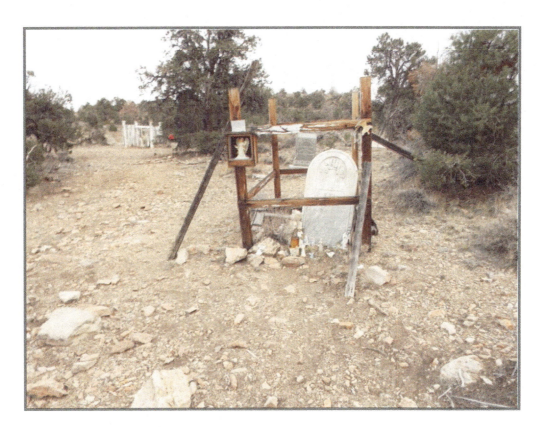

PINE GROVE CEMETERY

4

Wilsons Back in Mason Valley

The Wilsons, according to the records, returned to Mason Valley in 1902 after the sale of the mine. However, they had maintained their homes and ranches in the valley through the years they were in Pine Grove. Big changes took place in the 25 years they were mining. A town was established in the middle of the valley, first called Pizen Switch, then Greenfield and by 1894, Yerington. The newspaper, "The Yerington Rustler" boasted of having

DAVID   ABIGAIL

600 permanent residents and having several churches, an opera house, a fraternal hall, two hotels, four saloons, four general stores and a volunteer fire department.

The Governor in 1902, Roswell K. Concord, was the sixth to hold the office and the United States President, our twenty-third, was Benjamin Harrison. Communities had sprung up in Fallon, Gardnerville, Smith Valley, Reno, Carson City and most of Western Nevada. Roads had been and were being built, along with bridges to cross most rivers.

Most of the good farming and ranch properties had been acquired and the valley was beginning to fill. David and Abigail Wilson moved back to their original ranch near Wilson Canyon. The ranch house, according to Katie Buchanan, was an old saloon they moved in 1887 from Pine Grove and converted into a home.

By the turn of the century, the older Wilson children had married and started families of their own. Louisa had died Jan 30, 1890 at age 35; James W "Billy" was 43; Joseph I or "J I" was 41; George Washington "Mac" was 38, and Elizabeth J "Beth" was 19 and unmarried. During the mining years of Pine Grove the Wilsons also carried on their business in Mason Valley - Yerington.

David's brother, William Wilson, was born in Stillwater, Ohio January 16, 1827. He was one of the three brothers who originally came west to seek gold in 1850. He placer mined for gold on the Yuba River for a few years, then went to Virginia City during the Nevada gold rush. He partnered with Charles Wallace, better known as "Black Wallace," on Cedar Hill - where they discovered considerable gold.

A few years later, William joined his brother David ranching in Mason Valley, still yearning to prospect and, eventually, in 1866 discovering gold in Pine Grove. He and David partnered in the Wilson Mine which turned out to be a big bonanza. He then married Maria Jane White, April 5, 1874, of Scotland Co. Missouri and he sold his interest in their mine to his brother David in 1875 and moved to Carson City. Maria died less than a year later. William then married Elizabeth A Stewart, March 21, 1880 and they had two daughters, Jesse Martin and Jeanne Lamkin of Carson City. He chose to spend most of his final years in Pine Grove until his death, on January 11, 1911 in Carson City.

James, the oldest brother, was born in Ohio on May 18, 1824. He and brothers David and William started west in 1850, but he contacted malaria in the Isthmus of Panama on their way to California. He had to be left there until he recovered enough to travel. He later married Elizabeth Mary Ann Degraff, believed to be from New York, in 1844. They had five children; first William Wallace, (1848-1915), married Josephine Riggs Brooks and had two children; second Martha, (1864-1947), married P M Burner in 1872 and had four children; third James Monroe, (1856-1901), wife unknown and had seven children; fourth George Washington, (1858-1943), first married Elizabeth Peck and had four children, and then married Emilalee Underwood and had seven children; and fifth Abner Orvil, (1860-1924), married Margret Chriswell and had thirteen children. When James finally got to Nevada, he found his brothers partnered in a gold mine at Pine Grove. History tells us that he worked with and for his brothers in Pine Grove for some years. There was information found that James' daughter Martha and her husband Presley Bruner were temporarily in Pine Grove. No other information was available until the record of Jame's death on March 17, 1902, in Blaine, Idaho.

The oldest child of David and Abigail, a daughter Louisa Amilda, born in Missouri, Nov 12, 1855, crossed the plains along with 3 younger brothers to Nevada by wagon train in 1863. She lived with her parents in Mason Valley and Pine Grove until her marriage to George Plummer Sr. in 1871. They had one adopted son, George Plummer, Jr.. Louisa was an invalid for several years and though she suffered greatly, she never complained and was constantly caring more for those near and dear to her. She died in Mason Valley, Jan 30, 1890, at 35 years of age and is buried at Elm Tree cemetery.

David and Abigail's oldest son, James Wm. known as "Uncle Billy" to his family and friends, was a very important part of the Wilson Pine Grove operation during the mining years. On April 10, 1877 he married school teacher Mary Alice Stevens (1855-1922), known as "Aunt Mollie" from Michigan. They had four children, Daisy Hall (1879-1972); Fred William (1886-1912), never married; Beth L Ellis (8/12/91 - 10/31/86); and Amy Belle Brown (8/09/1889). Each of the four children were born in Pine Grove.

JAMES WM WILSON
"UNCLE BILLY"

Uncle Billy's great-granddaughter, Judy Ellis said, "While Billy was growing up, his best friend and blood brother was 'Jack Wilson', a Paiute Indian boy who took the name Jack Wilson and was treated like a son by the David Wilson family. Jack lived with the Wilsons and ate meals with them…."

Judy Ellis also said, "My great-grandfather, Billy, was also politically active and elected to four terms in the Nevada state Senate in the early 1900s. He was instrumental in the construction of the Nordyke House. This grand house was built from lumber from a mansion (some say the old opera house) in Virginia City and shipped by rail to Mason Valley. This building, (after 2000) is still standing and is located on State Route 339 in Yerington. It was restored by Tom and Judy Price to its original form and listed in the Nevada State Register of Historic Places."

Family genealogist, Judy Ellis, uncovered much of the rich history of the Wilsons, including that of her great-grandfather, Uncle Billy. His daughter, Beth Louise Ellis was married to George Ellis, the Superintendent of the Copper Belt Railroad in Mason

Valley. Billy's son, William G Ellis, a ship-to-shore radio operator in WWII for AT&T, and his wife Barbara welcomed a daughter, Judy Ellis, now a retired teacher and our genealogist.

Uncle Billy and his family lived for many years in the Nordyke House. He ran the family owned Silver State Mills, which was on the property. He was very busy as a farmer, rancher, mill owner, and legislator.

This Nordyke Ranch, as it was known in later years, had been sold by Uncle Billy, passing through numerous owners over the years and had seen good times and bad. Uncle Billy left Nordyke and moved to the Reno area. He died in Sparks, Nevada, December 12, 1930.

Nordyke

Nordyke House about 2020

Wilson Nordyke house Early 1900

The community of Nordyke, on the southwestern edge of Mason Valley midway between Mason and Wilson Canyon, got its name from the mill grinding equipment that the Wilsons had installed in their new grist mill. The little town of about 150 people had a train station for the Copper Belt Railroad and boasted of a Post Office in 1910. After 1914 the community slowly decline.

David and Abigail's second son, Joseph Isaac (9/03/1859 - 5/30/1954), was born in Missouri and came west by wagon train to the Nevada Territory with his parents, David and Abigail, when he was three years old. He became the most prominent and well-known of the Wilsons over his lifetime. He went to school in Pine Grove as a little boy. Joseph Isaac was also close friends with Jack Wilson, whose family worked for the Wilsons. He attended Heald's Business College in San Francisco in 1879 a completed a business course and also acquired a practical knowledge of civil engineering. JI, as he

J I Wilson

became known as an adult, owned and managed, along with his father and brothers, the Wilson Pine Grove Mine. For over 50 years he was very active and highly regarded for his many mining endeavors, his ranches running cattle, horses, and other livestock, and numerous business enterprises. In 1892, he built and managed for

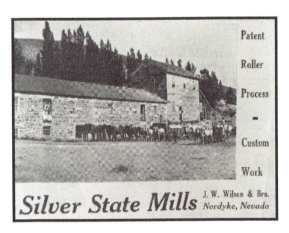

Patent

Roller

Process
■
Custom

Work

Silver State Mills J. W. Wilson & Bro. Nordyke, Nevada

NORDYKE MILL OWNED BY
J.W.WILSON AND BRO.

over 25 years the Silver State Mills in Nordyke, operating a grist mill to convert grain to bread-making flour. In 1918, his home at Nordyke was destroyed by fire so Mr. Wilson and his family moved to Yerington.

J I married Carrie Ella

J.I. talking with mill manager

Willis (01/26/68 - 09/03/25) November 24, 1887. She was nineteen years old when she married J I and was already a very accomplished young lady. She was the daughter of a well-known Methodist minister. Carrie graduated the Douglas Seminary in Genoa, Nevada and then graduated the University of Pacific in San Jose, California prior to coming to teach school in Pine Grove. Thirty year-old J I and his wife started their married life in the little mining town of Pine Grove. Their five children were all born after they moved to Nordyke. Only their first born, Joseph W and last born, Genevieve (Chapin) would live beyond their teenage years.

Carrie Willis Wilson

J I and Carrie had very illustrious years as adults. He was president of the Lyon County Bank for 26 years. He was president of the Walker River Irrigation District from its inception and for many years during its construction of two dams and reservoirs (costing over a million dollars). In 1902, he chaired the water board, which was responsible for distributing the adjusted water rights that came about after a seventeen year court battle that adjudicated farmers irrigation waters.

Around 1912, he acted as Receiver for the Nevada Copper Belt for eight years of settlement. About the same time he was president of Yerington Electric Phone Company and a school trustee and was elected to the state legislature at age 25. He was postmaster of the Nordyke Post Office for 15 years.

During her husband's career, Carrie also was very busy. Besides teaching school for many years at Pine Grove and mothering 5 children she developed a great interest in geology and mineralogy. She became known as, "the Woman Prospector". The latter years of her life were devoted to civic activities and work through The Woman's Club.

George Washington Wilson (08/09/1862 - 12/15/1927), was the youngest son of David and Abigail Wilson and was born in Iowa. He was about one year old when the family came west by wagon train. It was a strenuous trip for both mother and baby. He was reared in Mason Valley and Pine Grove but sent to school in Carson City. Like his brothers, he is a graduate of Heald's Business College in San Francisco, California. As a young man, Uncle 'Mack', as he was known by the family, was a mining partner and worker in the Pine Grove Wilson goldmine, from which the family extracted around six million dollars of gold bullion.

UNCLE MACK & LILLIAN

At age 21, Uncle Mack married Lillian B. Tillay, (1883), a native of California. They had two children, George Earl (03/19/1886 - 01/10/1943), and Queen Dukes (03/19/1884 -10/28/58), and an infant, Lenore, who only lived for four months. Queen and Earl were both sent to California to be "finely" educated. Uncle Mack, a staunch Republican, took active part in county politics and was elected to a four-year term as county commissioner. During his term they built 3 bridges and made many public improvements. "History of Nevada 1881" states, "He was not a member of any society or church, but took the Golden Rule for his moral standard. No man stands any higher than he in the community and he is not only prosperous but popular."

The last child of David and Abigail Wilson was another daughter, Elizabeth Jane, (01/26/1881 - 06/01/1947), born in

"Beth"

Pine Grove in 1881 to a 45 year old mother, 17 years after her youngest brother. What joy this baby brought to this mining family of 3 older brothers and one older sister! A family story tells, "David sent

Pine Grove School House Beth Wilson Student

Abigail with baby 'Beth' hauling the gold or bullion to the mint in Carson City, Nevada, assuming this method was safe from robbery because no one would molest a woman and her child!"

As Beth grew she went to school in Pine Grove. While this

THE TWO BETHS

was an adventurous life, it also must have been somewhat lonely as her brothers and sister were grown and starting their own adult lives. One of Beth's favorite friends was her niece, Beth Ellis, who lived part of the time at Rockland, a mine over a mile up the hill from Pine Grove. They managed to walk to see each other, though it was quite the journey. While Beth Wilson was the aunt, they were only a few years apart in age and began a lifetime friendship.

BETH WILSON

When it was time for a higher education, Beth Wilson's parents sent her to The University of Pacific in San Jose. Beth did very well in the fine art department, and became a very

proficient artist. When she returned to Yerington, she opened a shop to paint and sell beautiful oil paintings, charcoal drawings, portraits, and watercolor paintings. Many of those still exist among the remaining relatives and friends.

Beth Wilson

Beth Wilson Paintings

Beth (Wilson) McGowan 1905

The talented and beautiful Beth Wilson was a very eligible young catch for the valley bachelors looking for a mate. She came from a prominent, successful family. She had a very good education and the proper upbringing to be a perfect marriage partner. In the following chapters we will meet the young man that became the lucky husband to this, the youngest child of David and Abigail Wilson.

DAVID & ABAGAIL WILSON AND FAMILY - 1908

33

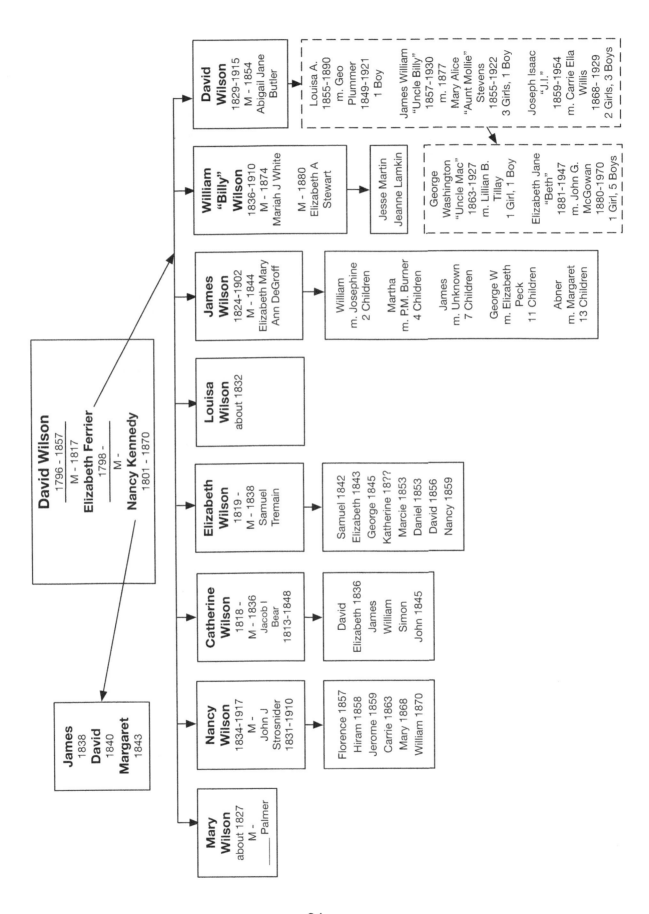

David Wilson
1796 - 1857
M - 1817
Elizabeth Ferrier
1798 -
M -
Nancy Kennedy
1801 - 1870

James
1838
David
1840
Margaret
1843

David Wilson
1829-1915
M - 1854
Abigail Jane Butler

Louisa A.
1855-1890
m. Geo Plummer
1849-1921
1 Boy

James William
"Uncle Billy"
1857-1930
m. 1877
Mary Alice
"Aunt Mollie"
Stevens
1855-1922
3 Girls, 1 Boy

Joseph Isaac
"J.I."
1859-1954
m. Carrie Ella
Willis
1868- 1929
2 Girls, 3 Boys

William "Billy" Wilson
1836-1910
M - 1874
Mariah J White

M - 1880
Elizabeth A Stewart

Jesse Martin
Jeanne Lamkin

George Washington
"Uncle Mac"
1863-1927
m. Lillian B. Tillay
1 Girl, 1 Boy

Elizabeth Jane
"Beth"
1881-1947
m. John G. McGowan
1880-1970
1 Girl, 5 Boys

James Wilson
1824-1902
M - 1844
Elizabeth Mary Ann DeGroff

William
m. Josephine
2 Children

Martha
m. P.M. Burner
4 Children

James
m. Unknown
7 Children

George W
m. Elizabeth Peck
11 Children

Abner
m. Margaret
13 Children

Louisa Wilson
about 1832

Elizabeth Wilson
1819 -
M - 1838
Samuel Tremain

Samuel 1842
Elizabeth 1843
George 1845
Katherine 18??
Marcie 1853
Daniel 1853
David 1856
Nancy 1859

Catherine Wilson
1818 -
M - 1836
Jacob I Bear
1813-1848

David
Elizabeth 1836
James
William
Simon
John 1845

Nancy Wilson
1834-1917
M -
John J Strosnider
1831-1910

Florence 1857
Hiram 1858
Jerome 1859
Carrie 1863
Mary 1868
William 1870

Mary Wilson
about 1827
M -
___ Palmer

34

5

Jack Wilson - Wovoka

Jack Wilson was a Native American, born in Smith Valley in about 1856. His father, Numu-Taivo, was a Medicine Man, which had a lasting impression on his son. Jack's mother and father worked for the Wilsons and made their camp nearby. When a teenager, he took the name Jack Wilson, but his Numu name Wovoka or "Woodcutter" came from the type of work he did on the Wilson Ranch. Young Jack Wilson spent much of his time with the Wilsons at the ranch. He was about the same age as the Wilson's three sons. The young Native American boy was accepted into their house and was exposed to considerable religious teachings from the family, including bible readings, evening prayer, grace at meals and other family devotions. Particular efforts were made by Mrs. Abigail Wilson to read to the boys some of the better known bible stories. He learned that the white man "had certain leaders, wisemen and prophets whom they revered and tried to live by their laws and precepts."

YOUNG JACK WILSON IN WORK CLOTHS

The following is from Appendix II, SETTLEMENTS AND ECONOMIC LIFE IN THE WALKER RIVER COUNTRY OF NEVADA AND CALIFORNIA, by Earl William Kersten Jr., 1961.

"Wovoka (Jack Wilson) was born in Mason Valley in about 1856. When he was a boy he was taken in by the David and William Wilson family, pioneer ranchers in Southern Mason Valley. He received bible training on the ranch and became Christian. Even after marriage Wovoka continued to work for the Wilsons, although he lived apart in his wickiup. Shortly before 1889, he became ill with a fever and was nursed by a neighboring rancher. During this illness, he had a vision. He related later that he had gone to heaven and had seen God. God revealed to him that if his people were good, lived in peace and worked, they would some day be reunited with the departed dead in another world, a world without pain or misery. God also gave Wovoka a dance. After his recovery, he began to preach this doctrine and to hold occasional dances.

HOPE SPRINGS ETERNAL —- THE GHOST DANCE painting by
Howard Terpning

The Ghost Dance symbolized the reuniting of the living participants with the ghosts of the departed dead. Wovoka's basically peaceful and benevolent Ghost-Dance religion spread rapidly from tribe to tribe in

the West and the Middle West. Among the Great Plains Indians the religion acquired a hostile tone, for it was claimed that when the ghosts of the dead were united with the living, great catastrophes would wipe the white man off the face of the earth. The abortive Sioux Outbreak of 1890 is attributed to the renewed militancy of the Sioux stimulated considerably by the Ghost-Dance Religion.

In spite of his fame, Wovoka never left Mason Valley. He continued his friendly association with the Wilsons and other ranchers. In every way, he was a peaceful and good man. He earned some income at the height of his influence by sending pine nuts, red ochre and other articles to Indian groups who used these for Ghost-Dance ceremonies.

Wovoka's dress and way of living symbolized the mode of Paiute adjustment to white culture. When James Mooney visited him in 1892, he was struck by the fact that Wovoka, like most Paiutes, wore white man's clothes, and yet lived in a brush wickiup and retained many other Indian ways. A broad-brimmed felt hat was secured on his head by a beaded ribbon. He wore a cloth shirt, coat and trousers and a pair of boots. Over it all, however, he draped a rabbit skin blanket. Inside Wovoka's wickiup were no white man's articles of furniture or cooking utensils. Mooney's impression was that the Paiutes spent their money earned from farm work largely for clothing, trinkets and rifles and ammunition for hunting. After 1900 the Ghost-Dance movement declined. Wovoka died at the Yerington Indian Colony in 1932."

Numuraivo's house at Pine Grove, circa 1880. Courtesy Nevada Historical Society

Beth Louise Ellis, granddaughter of David Wilson and daughter of James William 'Billy' Wilson, told the following story of her three uncles, who were David Wilson's boys, and Jack Wilson: "one day while playing in Wilson Canyon the three Wilson boys and Jack, cut their wrists, and mixed their blood and forever became 'blood brothers'."

Jack Wilson and his family worked for the Wilsons and each time the Wilsons moved, first to Pine Grove to mine and then returning to Nordyke in Mason Valley over 20 years later, Jack's family moved with the Wilsons. Judy Ellis added, "Beth Wilson Ellis and her sister Daisy handled his correspondence relative to his role as the 'Ghost Dance Messiah'." The sight of Jack Wilson's wickiup, below the old Wilson Nordyke home, has been fenced and saved.

Monument to Wovoka at the
Yerington Colony

WOVOKA

DEDICATION WOVOKA MONUMENT
1976 - YERINGTON

"Old Man Wilson"
aka Wovoka

WOVOKA

Jack Wilson (Wovoka) lost his following after the tragedy of Wounded Knee, at the Pine Ridge reservation in South Dakota. His prophesy, "a peaceful end to white expansion while preaching goals of clean living, an honest life, and cross-culture cooperation by Native Americans" never received its chance for fulfillment. He lived   quietly until his death, September 20, 1932 at the Yerington Indian Colony. He is buried at Schurz, Nevada.

6

Wilson Canyon

In the early 1800's, the white man traveled the area we know as Mason Valley on primitive trails. The area that is now known as Wilson Canyon was the only place where the river traversed the

Singatse Range of mountains between Smith and Mason Valleys. It was natural to name the area Wilson Canyon as the Wilsons owned most all of the land from Nordyke to the canyon. There were no roads or trails along the river that would allow passage through the canyon from valley to valley. To get between Mason Valley and Smith Valley, one had to use the Mason Pass trail or the more often used Hudson Pass. Much further south was the old Reese River road. In 1910, people finally gained the means to travel from valley to valley through what became known as Wilson Canyon. The Nevada Copper Belt Railroad built a railway to Mason and onward to Nordyke and, finally, through Wilson

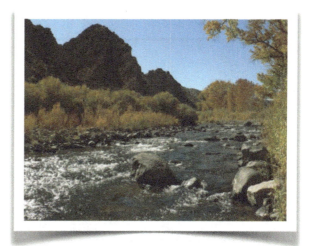

Canyon to Smith Valley. This was the first passageway through the canyon for human use. The rail line followed the Walker River west to Hudson in Smith Valley and then north to the Ludwig Mine which was the rail's terminus.

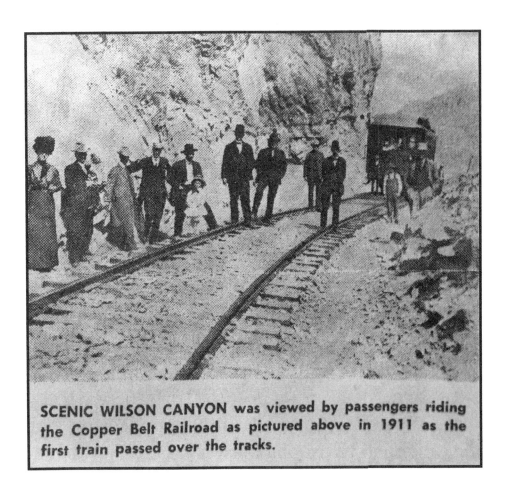

SCENIC WILSON CANYON was viewed by passengers riding the Copper Belt Railroad as pictured above in 1911 as the first train passed over the tracks.

ORIGINAL WORK CREW

AN EARLY AUTOMOBILE

GRAVEL ROAD - FENCE - TRACKS

YESTERDAY'S SWIMMERS

OLD TIME BATHERS

KATIES PLAQUE

WILSON CANYON MONUMENT
KATE BUCHAN, WILSON & MAE MCGOWAN

FISHING HOLE

AERIAL VIEW

THE OLD BRIDGE

Wilson Canyon Nature Trail

In 2011, retired Yerington school science teachers Steve Pellegrini and Arthur Shipley designed and physically developed the Wilson Canyon Nature Trail. It is a 3.5 mile hiking trail through the gorges of colorful rocks scattered with petrified wood remains. The hike goes through ancient volcanic canyons with many different geological formations. There is ample opportunity to see wildlife and raptors on this excursion. The State Highway directed the development with Pellegrini, Shipley, and others to enjoy the Nevada desert.

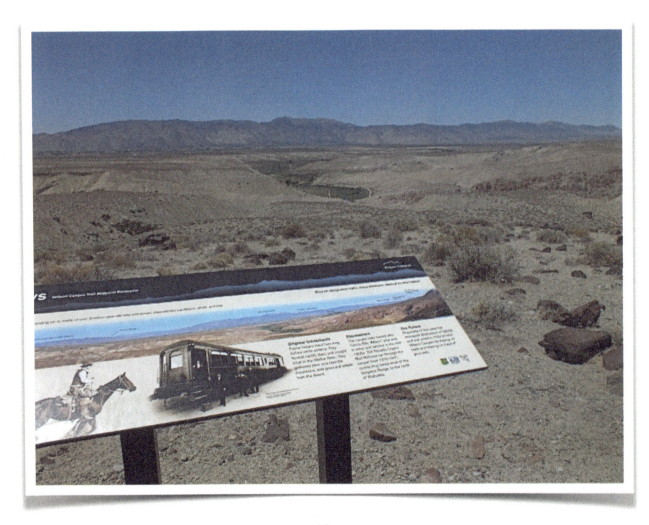

46

Paintings of Wilson Canyon
by John F 'Frank' McGowan

7

McGowans from Ireland to Pizen Switch

Our story now takes us to the "Green Isle" of Ireland to visit the other half of our family. Our tale begins with the John M McGowan family of Kinlough, county Leitrim in Ireland. John was born May 15, 1819 in Aughborrow, Ireland, 1 mile from Kinlow. He had 5 brothers, Michael, in the United States, Patrick, Terrence, William and James in Ireland and 3 sisters, Mary, Libby, and Ann in Ireland. In 1847, John M married Bridget J McGiven, born in 1826, and had a son, Terrence G (b. 1848 - 12/19/1907).

Family historians have written that John was a minstrel by trade. In 1850, according to his great granddaughter, Katie McGowan Buchanan, "It seems, that John got into a heated dispute with his English landlord and in the course of things conked him with a shillelagh. Thinking he may have killed him, he panicked and left his wife, Bridget, and son, Terrence, and jumped on a ship headed for New York, U.S.A. A few months later, learning that the landlord survived, John sent for Bridget and Terrence to come to the United States." They arrived in New York City in 1851.

The Irish Potato Famine (1845-1852) created a rush of migration to the United States where decent employment opportunities

prevailed. That created an overabundance of cheap labor in the eastern cities of the United States. This brought about a dislike for most Irish immigrants seeking work at any wage. It made living in the New York City slums very difficult. Trying to find a decent job was hard but John succeeded. Three more children were born to John and Bridget while they continued to live in New York; Ann in 1852, Catherine in 1856, and Mary L, year unknown.

Hearing that life was less crowded and land was more abundant farther west, they left New York. Their son, Terrence, was 21 years old in 1869 when they were living in Missouri. In the spring of that year, John and Bridget and family joined a wagon train on the California Trail heading westward, like so many other immigrants. They knew it would be a difficult trip, but the lure of free land and prospects of a bountiful life gave them the needed courage. They were confident the five months the trip would require would be worth it.

Wikipedia tells us the California Trail that the John McGowan family joined was first blazed by fur traders, scouts, and explorers, including Kit Carson, Joseph R Walker and Jedediah Smith. The U.S. Army and the topographer, explorer, and mapmaker John C Fremont was also one of the first into this western part of the country. Nevada become a state in 1864, so by 1869 the new state was five years old and had its first Governor Henry G Blazdel. Later that year, the first transcontinental railroad would make traveling coast to coast possible. The McGowans ventured West before its completion, and thus faced a most difficult task.

The first part of the journey followed the valleys of the Platte, the North Platte, and the Sweetwater rivers of Nebraska and Wyoming. This area would have consisted of mostly grassy plains, with a few small mountains and valleys. Then

the trail approached the rugged Rocky Mountain passes which presented the first extreme dangers. There does not exist any record of the route taken by the wagon train the McGowans were with in 1869, but it is suspected they made it over the Rocky Mountains at South Pass in Wyoming, as this was the lowest elevation of all and was the most popular for those headed to Nevada.

The route then headed through the City of Rocks in Idaho, then southwest to follow the Humboldt River near what is present day Wells, Nevada. The Humboldt, named after the well-known explorer, Alexander Von Humboldt, provided badly needed water and grass feed for the livestock, for the next 250 miles. The Humboldt Route, while it had water and feed, was also considered a very difficult part of the trip due to the alkaline soil, the sandy areas to traverse, little wood for fires except the very short sagebrush, and hardly any game to kill and eat.

John and Bridget, and their children with all their belongings, were growing weary of the lengthy journey, but still had many miles to travel to their destination. The wagon trail often had deep ruts they had to follow over alkaline stained soil while contending with alternating dust and mud. Travel was sometimes easier on top of ridges to avoid the brush and washes common in many of the valleys. Since the wagons tipped over easily, they were often dragged straight up hills, with multiple teams helping and skidding them down the opposite side. Many wagons had to be abandoned when they were badly damaged. It was very demanding and difficult work. The children of John and Bridget were of great help in their journey. Many had to walk or ride horseback, because there wasn't room in the wagon. By the end of their trip they had traveled over 1,900 miles to their new home in Nevada.

Arriving at the river's end at Humboldt Sink, they had to cross the very unpopular 40 Mile Desert. They loaded all the possible fresh water they could and started across the dry, sandy and alkali Nevada desert. Some could not make it and perished. Wagons broke and had to be abandoned. Some of the livestock died of exhaustion or thirst. However, the majority of the travelers did survive the 2 day trip through the heat and dust to finally make it to the Carson River. Here they would have found drinkable water and shade trees along with feed for their weary livestock and rest for all.

The McGowan family from Ireland, then took the Adrian Valley route south, covering the final 15 miles into Mason Valley. It was late summer 1869 as the folks from Ireland came into their final destination. The spot they chose was one mile North of McLeod Hill.

Mason Valley in 1869 presented its own challenges for the John McGowan family. The dry arid heat, relentless sunny skies, and the lack of trees (or much of any growth) away from the river was a stark contrast to Missouri. The surrounding mountains were also mostly barren with little or no growth. There were a few settlers here and there, but not many. In spite of all these new challenges, they resolved that this would be the place to take up acreage and settle. John and Bridget's dream was beginning to take shape: a new home in Nevada.

According to family genealogist, Judy Ellis, in Payson, AZ, "John M McGowan acquired 160 acres in 1882 through the Homestead Act and his son Terrence acquired an additional 160 acres in 1889." It is believed this land was about one mile north of McLeod Hill on what is now Highway 95A in Mason Valley. The end of summer required the McGowans to immediately start building a home so the family could have shelter during the coming winter. The first house in Mason Valley was erected in 1860 on the Hock Mason Ranch not very far from where the McGowans had settled. It was a 16X24 foot house with eight foot high walls of willows and adobe along with a roof of tules, but it

was burned by vandals soon after being built. The land also needed plowed and prepared with irrigation ditches to bring water from the Walker river about a mile east. Fencing was needed for their livestock. Food for the coming winter needed to be stored. The first store in Mason Valley was started by D. M. Geiger in 1863 and was near the east bank of the river about a mile away. The year 1869, when the McGowans first entered the valley marked the beginnings of a settlement that would become known as "Mason Valley." That year, W R Lee moved onto 160 acres, one mile east and about two miles south of the Geiger Store. Mr. E W Bennett, in 1871, moved his store from Pine Grove to Lee's property in Mason Valley. The Post Office also established there. A blacksmith and a saloon added to its size in 1872. The advantage of this location was its proximity to roads and trails traveling in most directions and it was near the river where decent crossings were possible.

The name Pizen came from the quality of liquor available in Downey's saloon. Charlie McLeod explains this early name in the following account taken from Earl William Kersten, Jr.'s 1961 dissertation, SETTLEMENTS AND ECONOMIC LIFE IN THE WALKER RIVER COUNTRY OF NEVADA AND CALIFORNIA.

The earliest name by which the little settlement was known was "the Switch" or "Pizen Switch." To reach it, people had to switch off from the mail trail. Pizen came from the quality of liquor available in Downey's saloon. Charlie McLeod continues his explanation of this early name as follows:

Pizen Switch

"Pizen Switch, as the story goes, received its name from the liquor in a saloon, which was constructed of willows and adobe. It was located near the present site of the City Hall of Yerington. Drinkers would partake of the tarantula juice and start to the Geiger Store about two miles north of town. Many of them would just make it to the store and fall off their horses. This was called "The dump." Part of the old wall or basement may still be seen on the east bank the old Merritt Ditch".

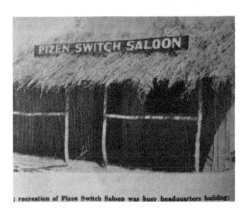

Replica built in 1976

Greenfield

Pizen Switch's name was changed in about 1881 as the town had grown to around 200 residents and a schoolhouse, Methodist church, five stores, three hotels, two saloons, two restaurants, three livery stables and three blacksmith shops. By 1890, according to the census, the population was 577.

Yerington

In early 1894 the name was once again changed to Yerington in an attempt to persuade railroad executive H M Yerington to run a branch line of the railroad in Wabuska through Yerington. The attempt failed but the name stuck.

OLDEST HOUSE—The oldest house in Yerington is the home on Yerington's South Main street (pictured as it is today) owned by Julia Lothrop. It was built early in 1871 by W. R. Lee.

The town of Yerington near the turn of the century, according to The Yerington Rustler newspaper, as stated on February 8, 1898, had several churches, an opera house and a fraternal hall to help serve religious and social needs. In addition, two hotels and four general stores were operating. A fire department had also been organized. The town had laid plans for several streets on a rectangle pattern and three blocks along Main Street were devoted to business. In February 1898 the first telephone was established.

While Yerington struggled for a numbers of years competing against the surrounding mining camps for supremacy, by 1911 the battle was over. Yerington became the county seat as the Dayton court house had burned. The new county court house was soon built on the corner of Main Street and Grove in Yerington. The Lyon County High School was built in 1909 in Yerington. During 1912 the city installed a new sewer system. More and more businesses were being established. The community had two banks. Doctors, lawyers, accountants and other professionals were establishing businesses.

"YERINGTON'S MAIN Street in 1917.

Mason

The town of Mason was founded in 1906 on the West bank of the Walker River about one mile south and about one mile west of Yerington. It was a mining and railroad town when the Nevada Copper Belt Rail Road (NCBRR) was built. The townspeople had a large celebration May 10, 1910 with a band and parade, boxing matches, a bar-b-que, and a baseball game to celebrate Rail Road Day.

Mason depot

The Bluestone Mine had a large copper deposit in the hills east of town. The NCBRR had its general offices, machine shops, freight yards, round house and passenger depot there. It served as a station for agricultural products, sheep, cattle and hogs raised in Mason Valley. Mason acted as a trading center for the miners and mine officials.

In 1914 Mason had a bank, a two story Hotel, many stores, saloons, a post office, brick schoolhouse, two churches, a laundry, a newspaper (The Mason Valley News), a hospital and a rising population. Mason did not, however, replace Yerington as the chief town in Mason Valley. The Yerington Times estimated the 1912 population of Yerington as 700 and Mason to be 400.

Mason Mercantile

There were several mines booming along with the Bluestone, with cars loaded for the Thompson smelter near Wabuska. During WWI, mines flourished, but after 1918 Mason steadily declined, losing the railroad facilities when the NCB was abandoned in 1947.

One room schoolhouse

8

John M. McGowan Family in Mason Valley

John and Bridget McGowan survived the first winter in Mason Valley as their new life was beginning to take shape. Their oldest son, Terrence, was 22 in 1870 and a great help to his 51 year-old father as they started farming their new land out West. Over the years, the McGowans slowly improved their home and farm despite their early challenges. The children did not have formal schools in the beginning, but as time passed there emerged one room schools in the valley. High schools were not available until after the turn of the century. More and more land was being acquired and the valley was starting to fill with settlers. The surrounding gold, silver and copper mines created a substantial need for farm product.

John and Bridget had three daughters, who were mentioned previously, in addition to Terrance. The girls were born in New York during the 1850s. Not a lot is known about them. It is believed they were on the wagon trip from Missouri to Nevada with the family, but very little is known about the third daughter, Mary L. Records show that the oldest, Annie E, was born in 1852 or 53, married Henry B Smith, and died June 6, 1910. They are both buried in the Yerington Cemetery. The second daughter of John M and Bridget J was Catherine, born in June of 1856 and died in 1904. She married John S Craig, born August 1836 and died December 1904. They are also buried in the McGowan plot in the Yerington cemetery. John Craig was a very industrious man of many occupations, including lawyer, saddle maker, Justice of the Peace, Postmaster, and a store and hotel owner.

In 1879, Terrence, age 31, married Louisa Hernleben, born January 1857 and died May 18, 1928. Louisa was born in Missouri; her family, the Hernlebens, had arrived in Mason Valley before the McGowans, having originally immigrated from Bavaria. They owned a ranch one mile south of modern day Yerington that became the Quilici Ranch. Terrence and Louisa had 8 children, William Roy born 1879, John G born 1880, Katie G born 1882, Henry C born 1885, Tessa W born 1887, Christopher born 1889, Frances L born 1892, and Terrence T born 1895.

TERRENCE AND LOUISA MCGOWAN

The McGowan farm was about two miles northwest of where Yerington is currently. Their children attended the Gallagher

Terrence, Louisa, and family

Country School that was close to the farm and easy to walk to. Louisa was busy teaching the girls cooking, housekeeping and clothes washing in their new Nevada home. Early on, John and Terrence spent a lot of time searching the valley for game birds and other animals the family could eat. As the years progressed, the availability of food was not much of a problem as they were raising their own livestock and had gardens. The amount of stores for staples increased with time also. These first years were very busy for Terry, Louisa, and family as they focused on getting a farm started and building adequate shelter.

The oldest boys, William Roy and John G, proved to be of great help to Terrence getting the farm established and producing crops that would support the family. Roy and John had to attend high school in Reno. A few years later, John attended Heald's Business College in San Francisco and then returned to Mason Valley to the family

Tessa John Kris Frances Louisa Ted Henry

farm, where he assumed its management due to his father's poor health and age. The family moved to MacKenzie Road, 7 miles south of Yerington in the late 1800's. It was at this location that the remainder of the family would reach adulthood.

William "Roy" (12/04/1879 - 12/09/1962) grew up in Yerington and moved to Los Angeles a few years after high school. He married Julia Etta Greeley, born in 1881, in Los Angeles in 1907.

Kate G, born in 1882, grew up in Mason Valley and attended school there. She married Mathew David on December 20, 1903 and mysteriously died August 11, 1904 at age of 22.

Henry Clay (1885 - 1930) married Susan Rose McGowan (1/1888 - 09/9/1953) in San Francisco and had a son Terrence Henry McGowan (11/26/1908 - 12/20/1987) who was married twice. He was first married in 1934 to Dorothy L Lockwood (8/04/1907 - 3/16 2004). They had two children, Terry Sue Myers born February 27, 1938 and Ross L McGowan born August 25, 1942. Terrence's second marriage was to Helen Evans (1925 - 2004) in 1953. They had two children Mark E McGowan in 1956 and Kirk McGowan in 1947.

ROSS MCGOWAN

One of the Mason Valley McGowan relatives that became highly known was Bay Area television award winning personality, Ross McGowan. He is the son of Terrence "Ted" Henry McGowan whose father, Henry Clay McGowan, was born in Mason Valley. Ross grew up with his sister, Terry Sue, born in 1938, in Cupertino, CA. going to Cupertino High School and San Jose State University. He was married twice, first to Heather Ramsey with whom they had two sons, Jeffery R, in 1969 and Kipp in 1974. His second marriage was to Pamela King, which ended in divorce.

He began his broadcasting career while attending San Jose State getting his degree. After an on again and off again career in radio he found himself in Seattle where he was hired by KIRO-TV to do fill in spots on the stations morning and night shows.

His big break came in 1977 when KPIX television hired him to return to San Francisco and co-host "The Morning Show" that Kathryn Crosby, Bing's wife, was leaving. Along with Ann Fraser he co-hosted the popular "People Are Talking" from 1978-1992. They also co-hosted "The Afternoon Show".

Starting in 1994, Ross was hired to be studio host of "Morning on 2" along with anchors Frank Somerville and Laura Zimmerman. During the next 16 years Ross did what he always thought he did best —"talk with people and interviewing them". He interviewed news makers, politicians, celebrities, common folks and all. Which gave 'Morning On 2" the tough edge on the news of the day.

With over 30 years on bay area television, Ross retired in 2009. He moved from Mill Valley to Hearldsburg, CA. where he no longer needs to rise at 3:00 AM to work. He is enjoying life in the heart of Sonoma Wine Country and culinary epicenter with friends and a little golf.

The fifth child of Terrence and Louisa was Tessa W, born in 1887. She grew up in Mason Valley and attended school there.

Tessa married Walter Wood, August 5, 1905, in a double wedding ceremony in the Methodist Church in Yerington along with her brother John G and Beth Wilson. A few years following their wedding the Woods moved to Northern California where Tess became a librarian and Walter was a music teacher in Arcata. They had two children, Truman and Louise (dates unknown). Tess and Walter lived out their lives in Arcata.

Walter & Tess

Howard & Louise

Christopher H (2/18/1889 - 10/22/1930) was the sixth child born to Terrence and Louisa, about the time they moved to MacKenzie Road. He attended The Barrett Country School, six miles south of Yerington. He went to high school in Yerington at the Lyon County High School. Chris married Veronica "Grace" Anfang from Colorado and they had three children.

Chris & Grace

Their first child was Gerald G (8/10/18 - 2/22/98). He grew up at the family ranch, attended school at The Barrett Country School, six miles south of Yerington and Lyon County High School

in town. As a young man he joined the Marines and saw action during WWII and the Korean War. Gerald was a district superintendent for Sierra Pacific Power Co. He married Ida Perry while living in Yerington. They had three children, Jason, who lived in Michigan, and two daughters, Judy Ellithorpe of Las Vegas and

Gerald & Ida

Sandra McGowan of Reno. Gerald and Ida were blessed with two grandchildren.

Gerald & Frank

The second child, Frank M (3/22/20 - 11/17/95) was born at the ranch on MacKenzie Road, attended the Barret Country School and high school in Yerington. He joined the Army Air Corps following the start of WWII and was a survivor of The Bataan Death March in the Philippines, receiving a Purple Heart and Bronze Star. He married Dorothy Martin (1/31/26 - 3/27/97) and had two children. Frank was Mayor of Yerington starting in the early 1960's and was a City Council Member and City Manager from the mid-1970s until 1988.

Dorothy & Frank

Frank and Dorothy's first born, a son, Timothy, resides in Lund, Nevada. The second child, Madeline Sanford, lives in Reno. Frank and Dorothy had three granddaughters and one grandson.

The third child of Chris and Grace was the girl they had always wanted. She was named Theresa after her aunt, and called Tessie. She was born April 26, 1925 and raised on the McGowan Ranch on MacKenzie Road. Tessie went to The Barret Country School and Plummer Country School in Mason Valley. She then attended Lyon County High School in Yerington. Her father, Christopher, died when she was five years old and her mother became the cook at the John McGowan ranch to support her family. Tessie and her cousin Katie, John and

Manuel & Tess

Katie & Tessie

Beth's daughter, became very close friends, which lasted for their life-times. Tess married her high school sweetheart, Manuel Barcellos (1/27/21 - 4/09/2015) on April 15, 1945 and raised five children in Yerington. Manuel was a truck driver when they first married and later bought and owned the Texaco distributorship for the surrounding area. Tess and Manuel led a very close life, never being far apart in their seventy years of marriage.

Their first child, Terrence, born in 1945, is a retired Army colonel, married to Sharon and lives in Fort Myers, Florida. Their second child is Delores Clewe. She was born in 1947, and is a retired school teacher living in Reno with her husband and travel companion, Press. The third child, another girl, Nadine Cozzalio was born in 1949. She is married to Ernie and is retired from the US Postal Service in Reno. James, 'Jim' was the forth child born in 1956. He is retired from the US Cooperative Extension Service and lives in Reno with his friend, Paul Devereuz. The last of Tess and

Manuel's children, Leslie Mueller was born in 1959. She is married to Joel and is still working in the television business in Reno.

Tess passed away September 9, 2016.

Jim, Delores, Manuel, Terry, Tess, Nadine & Leslie

Terrence and Louisa's seventh child, Frances L.(1892-1971) was born in Mason Valley on MacKenzie Lane at the McGowan Ranch. The last girl of the family grew to be known as Aunt Frank. She was married in 1914 to Dr. Scott, a dentist in Eureka, California and they had a daughter named Betty. Frances, later married George E Rees, (1884-1962) and they lived in Arcata, California.

The eighth child of Terrence and Louisa McGowan was Terrence T, born in 1895, on the ranch on MacKenzie Road. He would be known as "Ted" to most everyone. As the youngest child, Ted was loved and pampered by the whole family. He attended Barrett Country School and Lyon County High School in Yerington. Following some time in California, Ted and his wife, Willica, 'Billie', returned to Mason Valley where Ted's father was foreman of the famous Miller and Lux Ranch. In 1941, they moved to Reno with their children, Patricia and William Darrel. Patricia, born in San Francisco in 1924, was a soprano singer with the USO during WWII. Following the war she began her long and illustrious career as a home designer in Reno during the late 1950s. She married Wayne Wirsching and they had a boy and a girl. Pat died September 23, 2014 after a beautiful ninety year lifetime. William 'Darrel', (1928 - 2016) was born in Yerington, and schooled in Reno. He spent 4 years in the US Air Force, and had a long and successful 33 year career with Sierra Pacific Power Co. He was married to Roberta. They lived in Reno and had two girls, a boy, and one grandchild.

Billie, Pat & Ted

The story of Terrence and Louisa's second child, John G, is the focus of the following chapter.

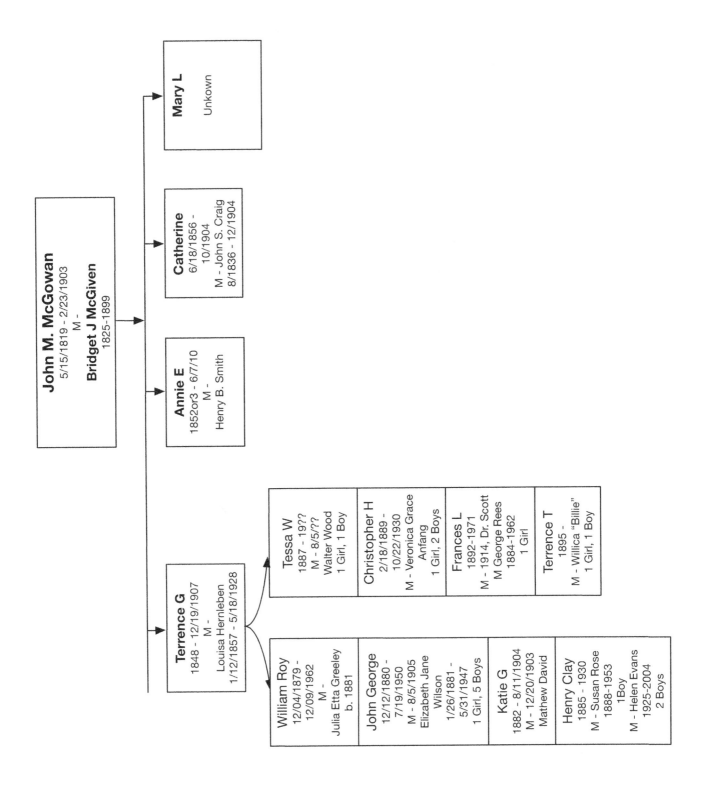

John M. McGowan
5/15/1819 - 2/23/1903
M -
Bridget J McGiven
1825-1899

Mary L
Unkown

Catherine
6/18/1856 -
10/1904
M - John S. Craig
8/1836 - 12/1904

Annie E
1852or3 - 6/7/10
M -
Henry B. Smith

Terrence G
1848 - 12/19/1907
M -
Louisa Hernleben
1/12/1857 - 5/18/1928

Tessa W
1887 - 19??
M - 8/5/??
Walter Wood
1 Girl, 1 Boy

Christopher H
2/18/1889 -
10/22/1930
M - Veronica Grace
Anfang
1 Girl, 2 Boys

Frances L
1892-1971
M - 1914, Dr. Scott
M George Rees
1884-1962
1 Girl

Terrence T
1895 -
M - Willica "Billie"
1 Girl, 1 Boy

William Roy
12/04/1879 -
12/09/1962
M -
Julia Etta Greeley
b. 1881

John George
12/12/1880 -
7/19/1950
M - 8/5/1905
Elizabeth Jane
Wilson
1/26/1881 -
5/31/1947
1 Girl, 5 Boys

Katie G
1882 - 8/11/1904
M - 12/20/1903
Mathew David

Henry Clay
1885 - 1930
M - Susan Rose
1888-1953
1Boy
M - Helen Evans
1925-2004
2 Boys

9

John George McGowan
Born in Lyon County, Nevada December 12, 1880, second son of Louisa and Terry McGowan
Married Elizabeth J. Wilson August 5, 1906. Died June 1976

Elizabeth J. Wilson McGowan (Beth)
Born in Rae Grove, Nevada January 20, 1881
Married John G. McGowan August 5, 1906
Mother of five sons and one daughter

Pioneer Marriage

During the time John G managed the McGowan Ranch he started to show a great deal of interest in the youngest Wilson daughter, Elizabeth 'Beth' Jane, the artist. They were seen quite often at social events around the valley. The rumor was that "love was in the air!" To no one's surprise on August 5, 1906, a large gathering of McGowans and Wilsons met at the Methodist Church in Yerington to celebrate the double wedding ceremony of Elizabeth J Wilson to John G McGowan and Tessa W McGowan and Walter N Wood, by Reverend T H Nicholas. Beth and John were attended by Genevieve Wilson, brides maid, and William Roy McGowan, Groomsman. Hazel McNeely was bridesmaid and Henry McGowan was Groomsman for Mr. and Mrs. Wood.

Following the wedding, a "sumptuous breakfast" was enjoyed by the bridal parties at the McNeelys. Soon after, the McGowans "took their departure for Reno and Lake Tahoe and the Woods took to the hills for a camping trip." Invitations were extended for a banquet the 15th of August at Spangler Hall to honor the "new husbands and their wives," with family and friends.

painting of
The Honeymoon Carriage

An old newspaper article of the wedding, a formal wedding notice, and a copy of the invitation to the reception that followed the wedding and their honeymoons.

Double Wedding.

On Sunday morning last, the 5th inst., John J. McGowan and Miss Elizabeth Wilson and W. N. Wood and Miss Tessa McGowan were married by the Rev. T. H. Nicholas at the Methodist church in Yerington. The ceremony was a quiet affair, only a few friends and the relatives of the contracting parties being present. Roy McGowan and Miss Genevieve Wilson and Henry McGowan and Miss Hazel McNeely acted as groomsmen and bridesmaids. After the ceremony congratulations were extended and a sumptuous wedding breakfast was partaken of at the McNeely residence by the bridal party. At noon Mr. and Mrs. McGowan took their departure for Reno and Lake Tahoe and Mr. and Mrs. Wood took to the hills on a camping trip.

Mr. McGowan and bride and Mrs. Wood are natives of Mason Valley, while Mr. Wood has been a resident of Yerington for a year or more. All are well and favorably known here, the brides being bright, intelligent and altogether charming young ladies, and they number their friends in this vicinity by the score. Everybody and the TIMES wish them a long and happy wedded life.

Invitations are out for a banquet to be given at Spangler Hall on the evening of the 15th in honor the newly-made benedicts and their wives. Those who have them are lucky and those who fail to attend will miss the greatest spread ever offered up to Cupid in this section of the country.

Newspaper Article

Mr. John G. McGowan

Miss Elizabeth J. Wilson

Married

Sunday, August fifth

nineteen hundred and six

Yerington, Nevada

At Home
after August twentieth
Yerington, Nevada

Printed Notice

MENU AND WINE LIST
TALLAC
HOUSE - LAKE TAHOE

Invitation

Typical of the times, there was always work to do on the ranch. The young McGowan couple were busy starting life together on Beth's father's ranch. The David Wilson ranch would soon be gifted to John and Beth and through hard work, perseverance, and the acquisition of additional properties, the ranch would grow to a very large operation known as the John G McGowan Ranch. The young McGowan couple were also busy producing children following their 1906 marriage and by 1915 they had five sons and eight years later had the daughter they so yearned for. The oldest son was Wilson Leroy, born July 26, 1908; then Jack Harland, born 1/08/1910; third was Howard Vernon, born August 11, 1911; then David Terrence, born July 14, 1913;

Young McGowan Family

fifth was George Sanford, born February 16, 1915; and finally, the daughter Katherine Louise, born June 20, 1922. The McGowan children and their families will be covered in a following chapter. John and Beth in their first years of marriage planted the mile long row of stately Lombardi Poplar trees that grew and became a

John and his banker inspecting the new potato digging machine (painting by Frank McGowan)

landmark at the south end of the valley for over 100 years. The McGowan ranch was diversifying and over the years, they developed a herd of beef cattle that were raised and fed on the ranch. They raised dairy cattle mostly for cream to make butter at Yerington Creamery with the excess milk for their pigs raised for slaughter at Peoples Packing Plant in Yerington. There was a large orchard that produced fruit for eating and canning for the ranch's dinner table. Chickens were raised to eat, produce eggs, and generate income through the sale of both chickens and eggs to the local grocery store. The crops were grain, alfalfa, and potatoes. In addition they raised a very large garden for summer produce and canning. They were among the first to own a new John Deere tractor, a new Caterpillar, a new International Harvester grain thrasher, a new hay bailer, and many more small farming implements. Over the years, there were many barns, cellars, corrals, pens, and miles of fences they built for improvements to one of the largest ranches in Mason Valley. All the while, they had

Stacking hay with family (painting)

to contend with the normal repairs and maintenance of a large ranch. John McGowan and his sons and daughter became quite adept at building and maintaining their ranch.

John and Beth were very well known in Mason Valley. They played music together (he the violin and she the piano) for

community dances and social affairs. For some time, John belonged to the Lyon County School Board and served as chairman for a number of years during their children's school years. John was active in the organization and development of the Yerington Creamery Association and served as president of the business.

Painting by Mimi Job of McGowan ranch house
with Mollie, Katie and Tessie by old Model T

Dave, Wilson, Molly, Aunt Grace, Lou, Howard, John, Katie. Jack,
Tessie, Marie, George and Beth

John was a member of the Methodist Church and a past master of Hope Lodge, 22 F & A M of Yerington. He was past patron of Naomi Chapter, Order of the Eastern Star, a member of the Scottish Rite Bodies of Reno and Kerak Shrine Temple. He was a lifelong Republican, a member of the Nevada Farm Bureau, and served as a director of the Mason Valley Bank.

Beth was also a lifelong

Beth (Wilson) McGowan 1905

Republican, member of the Methodist Church and was a member of the Yerington Lodge 22 Order of the Eastern Star in Yerington. She was a woman of strong convictions like her parents.

Katie, Dave, Howard, Jack, John, Wilson and Beth

A family incident brought back memories of her strong beliefs. Beth and John played cards with her niece Daisy Hall and her husband Fletcher in the evenings at their home on the ranch. Fletcher and Daisy were beekeepers. Fletcher chewed tobacco, which bothered Beth and she told him she thought it was a dirty habit. One night during a highly contested card game with Fletcher having a very large chew in his mouth and it dripping down his chin, he S N E E Z E D!!! The ensuing scene was very unpleasant and ugly!
After cleaning the tobacco and spit from all over the oil tablecloth, the game came to an abrupt end. Then the lecture of cleanliness, good health and respectable behavior began and continued until Fletcher and Daisy took leave for the night!! Beth required respect and she got it!

John's and Beth's children's stories follow…

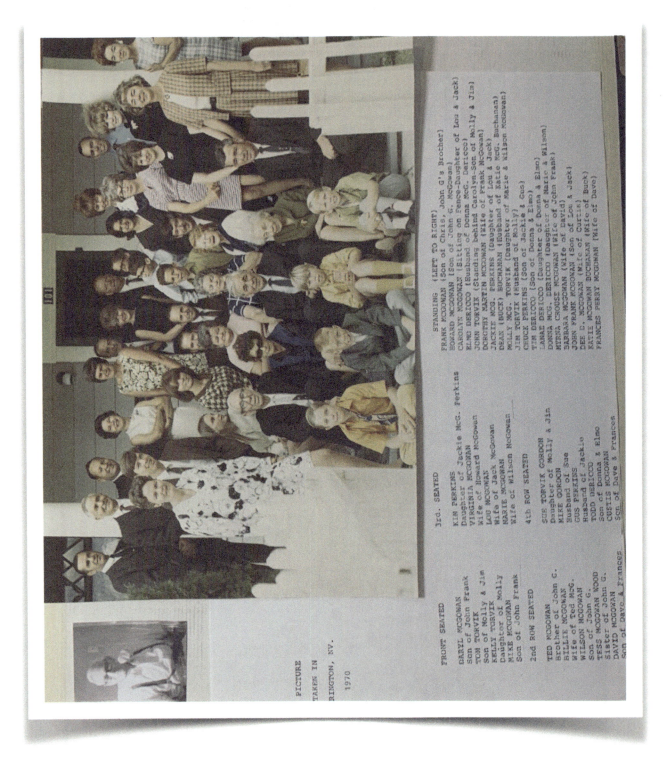

PICTURE
TAKEN IN
...RINGTON, NV.
1970

FRONT SEATED

DARYL MCGOWAN
Son of John Frank
TOM TORVIK
Son of Molly & Jim
KELLY TORVIK
Daughter of Molly
MIKE MCGOWAN
Son of John Frank

2nd ROW SEATED

TED MCGOWAN
Brother of John G.
BILLIE MCGOWAN
Wife of Ted McG.
WILSON MCGOWAN
Son of John G.
TESS MCGOWAN WOOD
Sister of John G.
DAVID MCGOWAN
Son of Dave & Frances

3rd. SEATED

KIM PERKINS
Daughter of Jackie McG. Perkins
VIRGINIA MCGOWAN
Wife of Howard McGowan
LOU MCGOWAN
Wife of Jack McGowan
MARIE MCGOWAN
Wife of Wilson McGowan

4th ROW SEATED

SUE TORVIK GORDON
Daughter of Molly & Jim
MIKE GORDON
Husband of Sue
GUS PERKINS
Husband of Jackie
TODD DERICCO
Son of Donna & Elmo
CURTIS MCGOWAN
Son of Dave & Frances

STANDING (LEFT TO RIGHT)

FRANK MCGOWAN (Son of Chris, John G's Brother)
HOWARD MCGOWAN (Son of John G. McGowan)
CAROLYN MCGOWAN (Sitting on Fence-Daughter of Lou & Jack)
ELMO DERICCO (Husband of Donna McG. Dericco)
JOHN TORVIK (Standing behind Carolyn-Son of Molly & Jim)
DOROTHY MARTIN MCGOWAN (Wife of Frank McGowan)
JACKIE MCG. PERKINS (Daughter of Lou & Jack)
DEAN (BUCK) BUCHANAN (Husband of Katie McG. Buchanan)
MOLLY MCG. TORVIK (Daughter of Marie & Wilson McGowan)
JIM TORVIK (Husband of Molly)
CHUCK PERKINS (Son of Jackie & Gus)
TIM DERICCO (Son of Donna & Elmo)
LANAE DERICCO (Daughter of Donna & Elmo)
DONNA MCG. DERICCO (Daughter of Marie & Wilson)
MYRNA CROUSE MCGOWAN (Wife of John Frank)
BARBARA MCGOWAN (Wife of David)
JOHN FRANK MCGOWAN (Son of Lou & Jack)
DEE D. MCGOWAN (Wife of Curtis)
KATIE MCGOWAN BUCHANAN (Wife of Buck)
FRANCES PERRY MCGOWAN (Wife of Dave)

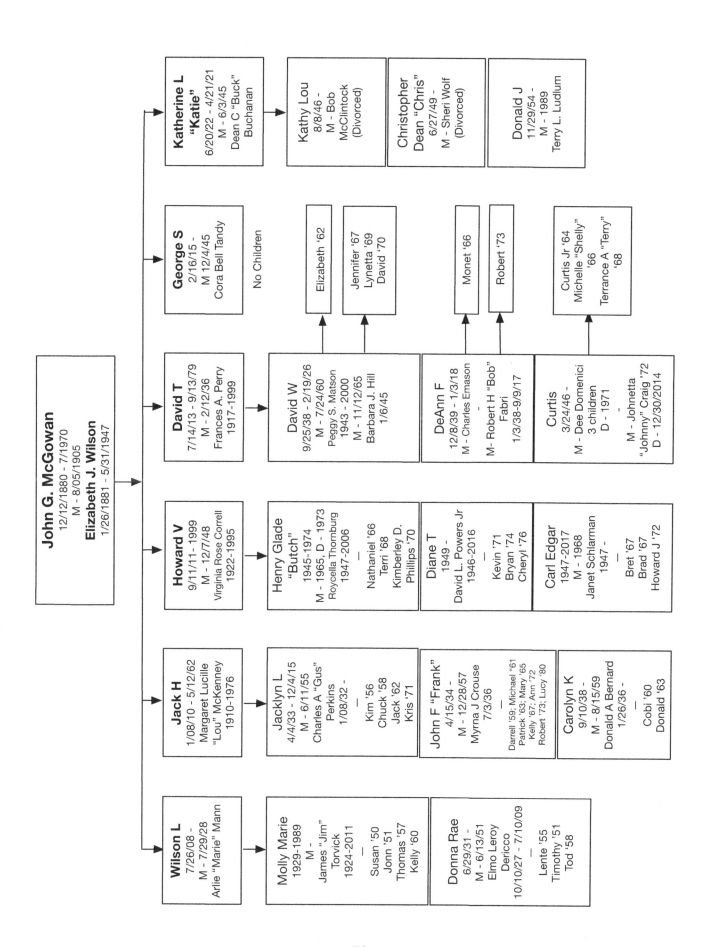

John G. McGowan
12/12/1880 - 7/1/1970
M - 8/05/1905
Elizabeth J. Wilson
1/26/1881 - 5/31/1947

Wilson L
7/26/08 -
M - 7/29/28
Arlie "Marie" Mann

Molly Marie
1929-1989
M -
James "Jim"
Torvick
1924-2011
—
Susan '50
Jonn '51
Thomas '57
Kelly '60

Donna Rae
6/29/31 -
M - 6/13/51
Elmo Leroy
Dericco
10/10/27 - 7/10/09
—
Lente '55
Timothy '51
Tod '58

Jack H
1/08/10 - 5/12/62
Margaret Lucille
"Lou" McKenney
1910-1976

Jacklyn L
4/4/33 - 12/4/15
M - 6/11/55
Charles A "Gus"
Perkins
1/08/32 -
—
Kim '56
Chuck '58
Jack '62
Kris '71

John F "Frank"
4/15/34 -
M - 12/28/57
Myrna J Crouse
7/3/36
—
Darrell '59; Michael '61
Patrick '63; Mary '65
Kelly '67; Ann '72
Robert '73; Lucy '80

Carolyn K
9/10/38 -
M - 8/15/59
Donald A Bernard
1/26/36 -
—
Cobi '60
Donald '63

Howard V
9/11/11 - 1999
M - 12/7/48
Virginia Rose Correll
1922-1995

Henry Glade
"Butch"
1945-1974
M - 1965, D - 1973
Roycella Thornburg
1947-2006
—
Nathaniel '66
Terri '68
Kimberley D.
Phillips '70

Diane T
1949 -
David L. Powers Jr
1946-2016
—
Kevin '71
Bryan '74
Cheryl '76

Carl Edgar
1947-2017
M - 1968
Janet Schlarman
1947 -
—
Bret '67
Brad '67
Howard J '72

David T
7/14/13 - 9/13/79
M - 2/12/36
Frances A. Perry
1917-1999

David W
9/25/38 - 2/19/26
M - 7/24/60
Peggy S. Matson
1943 - 2000
M - 11/12/65
Barbara J. Hill
1/6/45

Elizabeth '62

Jennifer '67
Lynetta '69
David '70

DeAnn F
12/8/39 - 1/3/18
M - Charles Emason
M - Robert H "Bob"
Fabri
1/3/38-9/9/17

Monet '66

Robert '73

Curtis
3/24/46 -
M - Dee Domenici
3 children
D - 1971
M - Johnetta
"Johnny" Craig '72
D - 12/30/2014

Curtis Jr '64
Michelle "Shelly"
'66
Terrance A "Terry"
'68

George S
2/16/15 -
M 12/4/45
Cora Bell Tandy

No Children

**Katherine L
"Katie"**
6/20/22 - 4/21/21
M - 6/3/45
Dean C "Buck"
Buchanan

Kathy Lou
8/8/46 -
M - Bob
McClintock
(Divorced)

Christopher
Dean "Chris"
6/27/49 -
M - Sheri Wolf
(Divorced)

Donald J
11/29/54 -
M - 1989
Terry L. Ludlum

10

Wilson L. McGowan Family

The first child to be born to John G and Elizabeth was Wilson LeRoy, on July 26, 1908, a proud occasion for the Wilsons and the McGowans. This was the first grandchild of the "Pioneer Marriage." For Terrence and Louisa McGowan it was their first grandchild. Wilson was a very strong and healthy boy. He quickly grew into the leadership of the fast growing family, as four more boys would be born by 1915. Wilson took to the rancher's son's role easily and really enjoyed farming and raising livestock. He learned responsibility and completed his jobs quickly and well.

WILSON

Wilson went to grammar school about a mile from the ranch house at The Plummer Country School. The property for the school was donated by his uncle, George Plummer. The first two years of high school were in Reno for Wilson. The last two were in Yerington at the Lyon County High School where he did very well academically and excelled at football and other activities.

Being the first son, a lot of responsibility was given Wilson. On one occasion he went with his father to the middle of the state to buy range cattle to add to the herd being established. Following

the purchase, Wilson stayed with the new cows, first on the train, then on horseback until they reached the McGowan Ranch. His father, about this same time, bought 400 acres from Frank Stickney that adjoined the ranch, for a total of 1,200 acres. The ranch was then raising 1,500 tons of hay per year. Wilson drove different horse and tractor-drawn equipment as a young man. He helped in the haying process alongside many Paiute men and women. The ranch fed all the workers on the hay crews three big meals a day. Over the years, the method of haying improved from small haystacks and derricks to large round haystacks of up to 100 tons each. Then the ranch starting utilizing the sidewinder rakes and the first hay bailers. Slowly the farm animals were replaced by modern farm equipment.

WILSON

After high school, Wilson attended Heald's Business College in San Francisco. The Great Depression was just getting started and changed many plans for many people. It became necessary for Wilson to return home after a year and try to help his father and brothers save the ranch.

MARIE

Frank & Madge Mann Wilson & Marie(mann)McGowan John & Beth McGowan

That was when Wilson, the handsome young rancher, met the striking, first year Smith Valley School teacher, Arlie "Marie" Mann. They married a short time later, on July 29, 1928, at the McGowan Ranch in Mason Valley. Following a two - week honeymoon camping in the Sierras, they returned to the ranch and started family life. Eventually they moved into

MOLLY AND DONNA

MOLLIE & DONNA

the "the little red house" where their two daughters were born; Molly Marie, on May 22, 1929, and Donna Rae, on June 19, 1931.

The mid 1930's were not very good times for the farmers of Mason Valley as the mines were all shutting down further depressing local farming. The McGowan Ranch was financed by the San Francisco Federal Land Bank and they were constantly

Donna, Molly, Beth, John
Marie, Katie and Wilson

wanting payment of the note. John G found it necessary to cash in his personal life insurance to acquire enough cash to pay taxes that were due and change the title on the ranch properties to avoid foreclosure. Wilson and Dave became the titleholders in 1937. During the ensuing year they refinanced and paid off the Federal Land Bank. Numerous innovations were deployed on the ranch to alleviate the debt and lower the cost of operations. They tried and were successful raising potatoes and dairy cattle. They sold the buttery fat to the Yerington Creamery for butter. Chickens were raised for eggs and meat to sell to local butcher shops. A large and very successful pig raising program got under way. The ranch had a herd of 1,000 to 1,200 beef cattle.

Wilson, Marie, and their young daughters spent a year leasing the Rosaschi Ranch on the East Walker River, just south of the Strosnider Ranch. They tried their hand at raising sheep. It was a new endeavor for the McGowans. Mostly due to the depressive state of the country, sheep raising was not a financial success for Wilson and his family.

DONNA, WILSON, MARIE & MOLLY

Molly and Donna traveled to Yerington Grammar School by school bus during their primary schooling. About the time they were beginning high school, the family moved to Lovelock so Wilson could raise potatoes for the war effort in 1944. The two girls were very busy in high school with cheerleading and other activities. They received very good academic scores.

The potato raising effort was quite successful for Wilson as he worked in partnership with brokers that helped sell the crop each year. At one point they were the biggest potato growers in the state of Nevada and had a large number of migrant Mexican workers in their employ. The Mason Valley ranch sold in 1946, so for one year Dave, Wilson's younger brother, went to Lovelock to partner with Wilson growing potatoes. Dave returned to Mason Valley after one year.

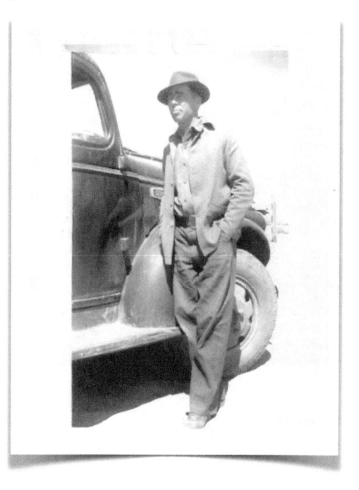

WILSON

Wilson found a fertile 320 acre ranch a couple miles north of Lovelock and purchased it, later claiming it was one of the best buys he ever made. Marie owned and operated a ladies' dress shop in Lovelock. Wilson and Marie lived in Lovelock until he "got into politics ."

In 1957, Wilson was elected State Senator from Pershing County. He became a popular politician and known as one that 'gets the job done.' This led to him holding the office until 1966. He then ran for Nevada State Controller and was elected and

served the State of Nevada from 1967 until 1982 under Nevada Governors Vail Pittman, Charles Russel, Grant Sawyer, Paul Laxalt, Robert List and Richard Bryan. Assemblyman Joe Dini - Yerington, described Wilson as "a dedicated public servant and a personal friend."

He went on to say, "Everybody looked up to Wilson." Mike O'Callahan, retired democratic governor while Wilson was State Comptroller, described him as "one of the finest public servants I've known." Wilson retired from government service in 1982, at age 74.

Wilson lost his wife, Marie, in January 1980, before he retired. He married Mae Morrison, Nov 9, 1980 in Carson City. They enjoyed traveling and golf during their retirement years. They bought a small home on Lake Mead in southern Nevada where they wintered for over 5 years, before they bought another small

MAE AND WILSON

home in southern California in a retirement community. During the autumn months they enjoyed traveling to different parts of California and Oregon. One year they flew to New Zealand and Australia for a wonderful three-week tour. Wilson died at age 93 in Carson City on September 10, 2001. Mae passed away on February 23, 2007.

Molly & Jim

Wilson and Marie's first daughter Molly graduated from Lovelock High school and went to College of Pacific in Stockton,

Molly

California to continue her education. There she met and fell in love with James (b 8/11/24 - 4/24/2011) "Jim" Torvick. Jim was the highly popular running back of the COP football team and roommate of the famous quarterback Eddie LeBaron, who later made NFL history. Molly and Jim married and started family life in Richmond, California, where Jim joined his brother George who was in the home building business

Marriage

during the 1950's. In the late 1960's they moved to western Nevada where Jim freelanced as a carpenter and Molly ran a clerical business in Carson City.

Molly and Jim moved to Fallon as retirement

early family

years approached. They loved being in the country and near their son and his ranching and cattle business. Molly lost a long struggle with cancer and passed away in 1989. Jim followed Molly in death on April 24, 2011.

The first child of Molly and Jim, Susan E Reynoso, was born October 15, 1950 in Berkeley and attended school in Richmond. She graduated from Heald's Business in Sacramento and was a court reporter for 35 years. Susan married Frank M Reynoso, an attorney and has three children. Frank had a personal injury law practice in Sacramento for over 49 years. He passed away on February 29, 2020, following a heroic battle with Parkinson's Disease.

Frank & Susan

Frank and Susan's first daughter, Renee Carlson, married Rich Carlson, and had no children. After several battles with lupus and cancer, she passed away in 2012.

Their second daughter, Dyanna Marie Longoria, is a homemaker and married to James (Jimmy) Longoria, a Cardiothoracic surgeon. They have three sons, Bryce, Jake, and JT.

Their son, Desmond Reynoso, works as a property manager. He is single and has no children.

Susan retired in 2013, and has been mostly involved in The Order of the Eastern Star, serving as a state officer in California in 2022, which involved lots of travel throughout California. During her free time, she enjoys traveling, hiking, reading and socializing with family and friends.

Reynoso Family

Mollie and Jim's second child, John J was born 8/29/51 in Richmond and spent his childhood in California. He moved to Carson City with his family, finished his senior year of high school, then attended the University of Nevada. Following his grandfather's footsteps, he became a rancher in Fallon. He married Vella Fairfax, January 24, 1981 in Fallon. She graduated from the University of Nevada with

John & Vella

a Masters degree in geology. They began with eighty acres and eight cattle, then added

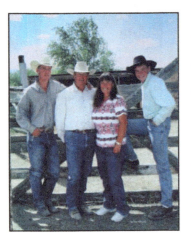

John, Vella & sons

property and cattle annually to the operation until they had a large red angus cattle ranch. They also raised alfalfa, corn, wheat, hay, and pasture. This enabled them to send the weaned calves each year to Harris Ranch in California.

They had three sons, James, (Nov 1983 - Feb 1988), Tyson, (10/22/85), and Mathew, (11/11/88). Tyson, following college, married Emily Ingram. They have two little cowgirls, eight and five years old, and many cattle and horses in their operation.

Mathew, after graduating from Washington State University, married Lena LaFrame, who graduated Washington State as a veterinarian. They own and run their clinic in Fallon and raise cattle and horses. They have two small cowhands, Callahan, four years old, and Tatanya, age two.

The third child Thomas W was born December 04, 1957 in Richmond, California. He attended school there until the fifth grade. The family construction business was closed in 1969 and they moved to Nevada. Tom finished high school in Gardnerville. He worked for his brother, John, ranching in Fallon until about age 25 and then started with Sierra Pacific Power in Hawthorne then South Lake Tahoe where he lived. He was married to Christie for 3 years but they divorced.

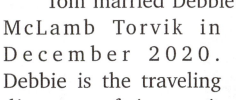

Tom

Debbie

Tom married Debbie McLamb Torvik in December 2020. Debbie is the traveling director of inspection for Man Mckay Associates of San Diego, CA. She has a son, Jacob Ward and one grandson. Tom retired from Liberty Power Company at South Lake Tahoe in 2020 and lives in Gardnerville, Nevada, where he and Debbie are enjoying golfing, traveling and lots of yard work.

Teeing off with deer friend!

Tom & Debbie

Kelly was the last born to Jim and Molly in 1960. As the family migrated to Nevada she attended Douglas County High School where she met her future husband Michael Garcia. They both graduated 1978 and were married in 1982. They spent several years attending college and taking bicycle tours. They established their careers in the construction industry first, then started their family. Molly Rae was born in 1992 with Donna Linzy following soon after in 1993.

Kelly and Mike

The Garcias built a home in

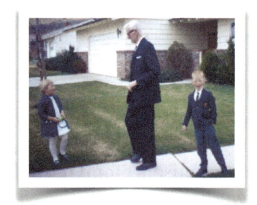

Kelly, G G & Tom

Bridgeport, CA, where Molly and Linzy were raised. Both girls graduated from Coleville High School. Molly is now a physician assistant and Linzy is an assistant professor at The University of Nevada. Mike and Kelly retired to a small home in Minden, NV. They still enjoy their bicycles and small town life.

Jenna Alexander, Molly, Kelly, Mike & Linzy

Donna & Elmo

Wilson and Marie's second daughter, Donna Rae, was born June 19, 1931 at the McGowan ranch in Mason Valley. She attended school in Yerington until 1944 when they moved to Lovelock. After graduating high school in Lovelock she attended the University of Nevada, earned a two year degree and later, a bachelors degree in education. She married Elmo L.Dericco, (10/10/27 - 7/10/09) in Hawaii June 13, 1951, while he was stationed there with the Marines. After discharge, he resumed his education at the University of Nevada with a degree in Education. In the 1955, they moved to Fallon where he joined the school administrative team and eventually became the Superintendent for Churchill County. Elmo

Donna

Elmo

was a popular leader of the Fallon school system. All the while, Donna became a mother three times while working in the Fallon school system. She retired after many years of teaching, most of which were spent in kindergarten and fifth grades.

The Dericcos were blessed with

Marriage 1951

93

three children. The first child was a girl. They then had two boys who kept them very busy. Raising three children in four years and following all their activities along with leading the school system and being active Catholic Parishioners and community leaders kept Donna and Elmo quite busy.

the Dericcos in later years

Dericco family tree

The first child of Donna and Elmo was born March 28, 1955, and named Lanae Marie. She was born in Reno. The family moved later that year to Fallon where Lanae attended elementary, middle, and high school. She attended college in Salt Lake City at Westminster College from 1973 until 1976 and attained a degree in education and administration.

From Salt Lake City, Lanae moved to Elko, Nevada and taught first grade from 1976 to1978. She then moved to Carson City and taught mostly first to fifth grade from 1978 -2008.

In 2008, she retired from teaching and still lives in Carson City. She enjoys volunteering at the swimming pool.

The second child of the Dericcos' was a son, Timothy John, born on June 6, 1957 in Fallon. He grew up in Fallon and graduated high school with a baseball scholarship in 1975, and spent two years at the College of Sequoias in Visalia, California.

He married Jerrie Plumhoff but was later divorced. They had one son, Wilson Elmo Dericco. He attended a gunsmith school in Susanville, California.

Tod Mathew, was the third and last child of Elmo and Donna. He was born September 12, 1958 in Lovelock, Nevada. He grew up in Fallon and graduated from high school in 1977. He went to Arizona Automotive Institute. Tod married Nancy in 1989 and they were later divorced. Tod has one son, Zachary Benjamin. Zachary has two daughters, Olivia Rae and Tatum Rose. Zachary works for the Bureau of Land Management..

11

Jack H. McGowan Family

John and Beth's second child was born January 8, 1910 at the ranch. They named him Jack Harlan McGowan. He was in poor health through much of his life. Both Jack and his older brother

Wilson were infected by Infantile Paralysis when they were young. It had severe effects on Jack, paralyzing parts of his body, which led to a lifetime deformity. As a child, Jack attended Plummer Country School which was located a mile from the McGowan Ranch house. He went to Lyon County High School in Yerington. As a teenager, he

Jack

Jack

worked on the farm with regular farm boy chores, helping with the haying and grain threshing during the summer months.

Following high school, Jack went to the University of Nevada for a year. He met and later married Margaret Lucille (Lou) McKenney on October 25, 1931. She was from Loyalton, California and graduated from the University of Nevada with a 2-year teaching degree. She was

Lou

teaching in Smith Valley and living with the Mann family. Due to a stubborn streak in Jack,

they were married three times, once by the Fallon Justice of the Peace, a second time by the Catholic priest in Yerington, and a third time by the Methodist minister in Yerington.

In their early years of marriage, Jack and Lou lived in numerous places in Mason Valley. They first lived at the McGowan Ranch, where two of their three children were born. Jacklyn Lucille was born April 4, 1933 and John F 'Frank' was born a year later on April 15, 1934. They then moved to Yerington and

Frank & Edith McKenney
Loyalton

rented a house on Nevada Street from Jack's relatives, Fletcher and Daisy Hall. From there they rented a few blocks north on the corner of Nevada and Littell Streets. Their next

proud grandparents

move was back to the McGowan Ranch and the remodeled Plummer Country Schoolhouse that cousin Fred Strosnider helped Jack remodel into a home. On September 10, 1938 their third child, Carolyn Kay, was born in their newly remodeled home. Their final move to 101 West Street in Yerington happened in 1940. The beautiful little two story home surrounded by a picket fence was just two blocks

Carolyn

Frank, Carolyn, Jacklyn
and Blacky

west of the Lyon County courthouse, where Jack was employed as deputy sheriff. This would be their home for the next 35 years until Lou's death on April 12, 1976.

The move back into town proved to be very good for their children. There were many families living in the neighborhood, the Rifes, the Aiazzis, the Perkins, the Recanzones, the Hillyguses, the Hatches, the Pistones and many more close by. Theirs was one of the most densely populated areas in town. It was only a six or seven block walk to school. The edge of town was just behind the McGowan home and provided open spaces for the children to play all their outdoor games. Those were the days before television, so the outdoors was supreme. There was football, basketball, bike riding, roller skating, fort building, playing Hide and Seek, Kick the Can, Ante Ante Over, and all the usual favorites that kids played. Building

Jacklyn, Frank Carolyn

tree houses with all their fathers' scrap lumber was also a big favorite pastime. Parents knew their kids were always within a "holler" somewhere in the neighborhood. Most families grew gardens and raised a few chickens. Gasoline was rationed, but most families couldn't afford to travel far anyway. A lot of boys had lawn mowing

Frank, Lou Jackie, Carolyn and Jack

jobs that provided spare cash for a soda or milkshake at the F & B Soda Fountain down by the courthouse.

The country was in the throes of the Great Depression and the Second World War was being fought worldwide. Many of the families during the Second World War didn't have a father at home, as he was off fighting the war. Jack tried to enlist in the Seabees in Utah with a group of men from Yerington, but he was rejected due to his deformities from infantile paralysis. He was very pleased with the deputy sheriff position but would have liked to do his part in the war effort.

Sometime near the middle of WWII, Jack contracted tuberculosis and was confined to a bed immediately. He had a severe case and was sent to different sanitariums in the high Sierra Mountains near Colfax and Weimar, California to try to stop its advance. There was no known cure for tuberculosis at that time and many cases were fatal. In 1950, at a hospital in San Jose, he had an operation to remove the diseased parts of both his lungs that had been damaged beyond repair. This saved him and added more than ten years to his life. During these years he became a New York Life agent and managed, with Lou's help, to add to the family income. In the beginning of Jack's bout with tuberculosis, Lou returned to teaching school at Yerington Elementary as a first grade teacher. Jack succumbed on May 12, 1962. Lou continued to teach until her retirement in 1974. In her sixties, she returned to the University of Nevada and completed her four-year teaching

Lou

degree as a matter of pride. During the years that followed, Lou continued to teach and traveled internationally during her summer vacations.

In 1974, Lou married fellow schoolteacher Donald Dallas. They traveled the United States and Canada in their Winnebago motor home for many months before her death April 12, 1976.

Lou

Lou & Don

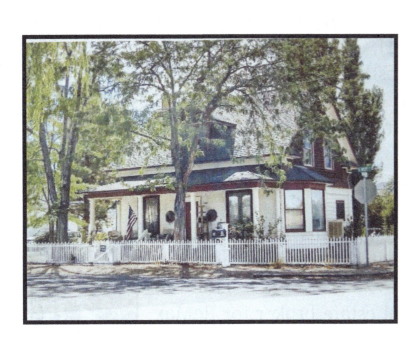

101 West Street Yerington, Nev.

Carolyn, Frank & Jacklyn 2020

Jackie and Gus

Jack and Lou's first child was born at the McGowan Ranch April 4, 1933 and named Jacklyn Lucille. 'Jackie' became the first

grandchild of Lou's McKenney family and the third of the McGowans. Jackie was a quick learner and as a very young child she learned to read. When she was seven, the family moved into Yerington. Jackie was a very active little girl and quite the tomboy, excelling not only as the best female horseshoe pitcher around, but also as an excellent softball pitcher. She excelled academically, graduating high school with a Harold's Club

Jackie

Scholarship to the University of Nevada, where she again graduated with honors. Jackie married Charles A (Gus) Perkins on June 11, 1955 in Yerington. They

moved to Reno and had four children, Kim E, Charles H, Jack E, and Kristen A. Until the kids were mostly raised, Jackie was a stay-at-home mother. Graduating Nevada, Gus was an appraiser for First National Bank of Nevada for over 33 years, becoming an Assistant Vice President. He continued appraising until retirement. Gus was University of Nevada Alumni President in the 1970's. As her children

Jacklyn & Charles

grew, Jackie became a real estate broker for ReMax of Reno and built a sizable clientele.

Gus and Jackie loved the outdoors and

Jackie

almost always owned a tent, trailer or motorhome to enjoy traveling, camping, and the outside world. They both had a high regard for education and made sure each of the children had an opportunity to attend college. The University of Nevada, Reno, hosted their children as they each furthered their education.

Young Perkins Family

Chuck, Kris, Diana, Mitch & Kim
Gus and Jackie - seated

103

Kim

Gus and Jackie's oldest child, Kim Elizabeth, was born June 7, 1956, married Dr. Mitchell Miller on May 8, 1982, after she graduated from Nevada. They lived for many years in Elko, Nevada while Mitch was a doctor of internal medicine at the local clinic. They returned to Reno in 2008, and Mitch retired in 2016. Kim and Mitch have three children, Brittany, born in 1989 in Spokane, WA, then boys G Ryan (b. 1986) and Jordan (b. 1989) both in Elko, Nevada. Kim and Mitch have three grandsons.

Kim & Mitch

Brittany - Jordan - Ryan

Chuck

The second child of Jackie and Gus is Charles H (Chuck) was born on March 15, 1958. He was raised in Reno. Chuck attended Lassen College and the University of Nevada and was a firefighter for the Nevada Division of Forestry from 1981 until retiring in 2008. Chuck and his first wife, Becky have a daughter, Lyndsey. His second wife, Beverly (Bev), is a CPA in private practice.

Chuck & Bev

They have been married 34 Years. Chuck has one granddaughter. He enjoys spending his retirement doing family carpentry projects, poetry writing, and sailing.

Lyndsey - London

Jack

The third child of Jackie and Gus Perkins, a son Jack E, was born in Reno on November 9, 1962. While attending the University of Nevada in Reno, he met Diana Barlow and they married in 1988. Following graduation from Nevada, Jack and Diana had careers in industrial automation and IT respectively.

Jack developed a passion for running and exercise. Starting with short jogs, then expanded to full marathons. He traveled all over the country to participate in marathons. Some of these were the Boston Marathon, the New York Marathon and the Death

Jack & Diana

Diana & Jack

Valley Marathon.

They are currently retired, living in Reno, and enjoy camping in their travel trailer throughout the United States. They also enjoy exploring other parts of the world and have frequently traveled internationally.

Jack and Diana have two grown children, Jamie who lives in Arizona and Rachel who lives in Reno.

Kris

The last child of Jackie and Gus Perkins, Kirsten A (Kris), was born in 1971 in Reno. She attended Reno schools and graduated from the University of Nevada, Reno. She married William Layman and had two boys, Andrew and Devin. Kris and William subsequently divorced.

Kris, Andrew & Devin

Kris is a realtor with REMAX Professionals which she joined to work with her mother a number of years ago.

Kris followed in her father's footsteps as President of the University of Nevada Alumni Association in 2018. Kris has been a big fan of the Wolf Pack athletic teams over the years and is very active in the Reno golf scene.

CHUCK - KRIS - JACK
107 JACKIE - KIM - GUS

Frank and Myrna

Jack and Lou's second child, John F 'Frank' McGowan, born April 15, 1934 at the McGowan ranch house in Missouri Flat. He was the first grandson of John and Beth McGowan. Soon after his birth, Jack and Lou lived in the remodeled Plummer schoolhouse. They moved to Yerington when he was six years old, and Frank attended grammar and high school there. He went to the University of Nevada, Reno for two years prior to joining the

Frank

Air Force. On December 28, 1957, Frank married Myrna J Crouse, born July 03, 1936, in Yerington while on leave from the Air Force. Following discharge, in 1958, Frank joined his father, Jack, with New York Life for a career of over fifty years. He earned many honors and recognitions from his company and the

Marriage

industry. Frank was also a community leader and large property owner in Yerington. He was voted 'Man-of-the-Year' following Yerington's 1976 U.S. Bicentennial celebration, a nine day community affair Frank organized. It was the largest celebration of the bicentennial in the state of Nevada.

Myrna and Frank raised their family of eight in Yerington. In the early years, Myrna

Myrna

was kept busy with their large family, but as the children grew older, she joined Frank in their business endeavors. She belonged to numerous community organizations and was the leader in the Catholic Church's religious education programs for a number of years. Frank and Myrna enjoyed traveling to different parts of the United States and internationally. After retiring, golf was a passion for a while, even owning a home in Arizona. They now live in Sparks, where Frank follows his lifetime hobby of landscape painting.

Dominique, Jonathan, Darrell, Susan & Hunter

Their first child, Darrell J, born August 30, 1959, completed degrees at UNR and the Franciscan School of Theology in Berkeley. He married Elizabeth DiTomaso in 1988. They had two children, Dominique and Jonathan. Darrell was a church pastor, chaplain, and funeral celebrant. Darrell and Liz divorced in 2012. He married Susan Britton in Hawaii, in 2018. He and Susan are now retired. Susan has one son, Hunter Britton.

Mike & Irene

Their second child, Michael D was born June 14, 1961, married Irene Aanerud, June 03, 2000. Irene had three children from a previous marriage, Michelle, Lindsay, and Nichole. Mike and Irene have three grandchildren. Mike is a tool and die machinist and master repairman employed by the Firestone Walker Brewing Co in Paso Robles, California.

Patrick & Lara

Patrick J was born June 15, 1963. He moved to Seattle, Washington after graduation from the University of Nevada. He married Lara Saario, May 10, 2003. Their children, Amelie and Ethan, are both in school in Seattle, Washington. Patrick had a very successful career as a research scientist with different international pharmaceutical companies in human cancer research. Lara is currently a Senior Vice President for Tatari , Inc. in Seattle.

Mary & Larry

Mary C was born December 17, 1965, and was Frank's and Myrna's first daughter. She married Larry Bright July 17, 1993 at Lake Tahoe. They had a daughter, Justine, and son, Zachary, in Portland OR. After earning her Masters in Counseling Psychology, she became a full-time therapist in Reno. Larry's three children from his previous marriage are: Ed Bright - Denver CO, Vicki McGregor - Martinez, CA, & Charleen Moore - Visalia, CA. Larry passed away on August 01, 2014 from a five year battle with cancer.

Kelly C was born April 12, 1967, following graduation from the University of Nevada. He married Lourdes Munoz on June 18, 1994. They had two girls, Ellise born 1995, in Yerington and Eviana after moving to Carson in 2003. Kelly is with the Nevada State Department of Water Resources and Lourdes works with the Carson School District. They are both very active with St. Teresa's Catholic Church in Carson City.

Ann & Rob

Ann T was born March 04, 1972, married Robert Bray in Reno on January 08, 1994. They have three children, Jacob, Joseph, and Julie. Ann, with education masters degrees from the University of Nevada, is an elementary principal in Sparks, Nevada. Rob, also with a Masters degree from Nevada, is a manager for Custom Ink.

Robert , Andres & Jeannine

Robert J, born July 14, 1973, after the University of Nevada, married Jeannine in Portland, OR on Dec 14, 2000 and have a son, Andres. Robert was a Vice President with Mattress Firm, living in Texas, and is now with Square Inc. and works from Sparks, NV. Jeanine, graduated with honors from Harvard University, is a CPA and owns a cross-stitch design company, (Blue Flower Stitching).

Lucy, Hailey, Aryana & Alex

Lucille Irene was born June 16, 1980 in Carson City. She is currently engaged to Matt Shermand and lives and works in Fernley. Lucy has three daughters, Alexus Kay McGowan, Hailey Jean McGowan and Aryana Gaylene Templeton/ McGowan.

Darrell - Frank - Myrna - Patrick - Mike - Lucy - Mary - Kelly - Ann - Robert

Carolyn and Don

Carolyn Kay was the third child of Jack and Lou. She was born September 10, 1938, in Yerington. She became the

Carolyn

'Neighborhood Traveler' and favorite wandering little blonde-haired child. The Rifes, Hatchers, Reconzones, Aiazzis, Stevens and others were all familiar with her. Carolyn attended school in Yerington and had many friends. Upon graduation she attended the University of Nevada and earned a two year Degree in education to teach school. Carolyn married Donald A.Bernard on August 15, 1959 in Yerington. They live in Reno where she was an elementary school teacher and Don was a Trust Officer for First National Bank of Nevada. They had two children, Cobi Lou Hess, born November 22, 1960 and

Donald A, July 12, 1963, each born in Reno. As time progressed, Carolyn stayed home to raise children and Don became a stock broker and investment counselor. The Bernards over time became community leaders. Carolyn returned to the University of Nevada to graduate simultaneously with her daughter. She was president of The Assistance League of Reno for eight years and served on their National Board. She has served for thirty years, five as Chairman, of the Hawkins Foundation. Together, she and her husband Don serve on a number of philanthropic trusts in Western Nevada.

Donald is Chairman of the Estelle J Kelsey Foundation. He has served on a number of community organizations and boards and is currently on the board of directors of RENOWN Hospital. In addition, the Bernards have become quite well known as property investors over the years in Nevada. In their latter years they have enjoyed considerable international travel. For many years they both were active golfers.

Bernard Family

The first child of Donald and Carolyn was daughter, Cobi Lou, born November 22, 1960 in Reno. She attended school in Reno and graduated from the University of Nevada where she met and fell in love with her future husband, Scott Hess. They married on May 26, 1984. Cobi and Scott live in Laguna Niguel, California where Scott is a contractor and entrepreneur. They have three daughters. Ashley and her husband Ian Hanes have two daughters, Hailey is married to Eric Keoni, and Kelsey is still single.

Cobi - Scott

Ashley - Ian

Hailey - Eric

Kelsey

The second child of the Bernards was Donald A II, born in Reno July 12, 1963. "Don" went through the Reno Schools and graduated from Nevada. While attending the University he met and fell in love with Sallie Nelson and they were married March 31, 1990. He joined his father as a financial advisor in 1988. Don is currently Sr. Vice President with Stifel in Reno. Sallie is a Dental Hygienist. Sallie and Don have three children. The oldest Brooke, born in 1992, teaches eighth grade at Billinghurst in Reno. Donald A III, born in 1994, is Assistant Manager and VP along with his Father at Stifel in Reno. Collin, born in 1996, is a Real Estate Investor and Agent with Coldwell Banker in Reno.

Sallie & Don

Don - Sallie - Donald - Brooke - Collin

Frank - Myrna - Don - Carolyn - Jackie - Gus

12

Howard V. McGowan Family

On the 11th of September, 1911, a third son, Howard Vernon, was born to John and Beth at the McGowan ranch. He was a healthy boy with lots of energy. Beth was quite busy with three young boys, keeping up with them and helping them stay out of mischief.

John was trying to farm the existing acres and acquire new land to level and ready for new crops. Howard and his brothers grew quickly and soon became their father's good helpers. They were quick to learn the chores of young farm boys. Howard matured and soon was a teenager working in the summer season, mostly helping with the haying. There was also cowboy work tending the ranch's cattle as they ranged from the Missouri Flat area to Bald Mountain to Black Mountain to Mount Grant to the Pine Grove Hills. The McGowans also ranged cattle in the Wilson Canyon area. At the ranch there were a multitude of jobs that required workers. There was livestock to feed, cows to milk, chickens to tend and irrigating to do.

Howard

Howard grew fast in this atmosphere. He was known for having a mind of his own. A story about him and his father was told many

117

times over the years. It seems that he had been working outside while the family had company. Finishing his work he came into the ranch house to join the festivities. His father, noticing he had his hat on said, "Take off your hat." To which Howard replied, "No!" John, becoming quite impatient with him, answered, "Well do something with it!" So Howard threw it across the room of guests and walked over to it on the floor and jumped on it with both feet!

Howard was a bright boy and attended Plummer Elementary Country School and Lyon County High School in Yerington and received very good grades. His father John, wanted Howard to attend the University of Nevada, Reno. Economic times were very tough and farms were feeling the squeeze. Though the Great Depression was in full swing, somehow a way was found to send Howard to college.

One of the boys' favorite projects each year after bringing in the harvest was cutting wood for heating and cooking at the ranch. The boys enjoyed this week-long outing in the mountains around Sweetwater Canyon. They always looked forward to camping out in the hills, roughhousing and hunting deer and sage hen. The giant pile of wood that was cut and hauled back to the ranch was almost as high as the ranch house itself. Then there was the cutting and splitting of all these pieces of pine. During the 1930s, this led to a very unfortunate accident that occurred to Howard! Back at the ranch while cutting and splitting the wood, Howard somehow cut part of his right hand off with a circular saw powered by a farm tractor. The cut was so severe that he had to be taken to San Francisco where, fortunately, they saved part of his hand and arm. It was a life changing event for Howard. He endured many further surgeries over subsequent years.

Howard showed quite an aptitude for invention. There was a period when they arranged a space for him to study and create new things. At one point following World War II, he had almost completed his invention of a patentable automatic automobile transmission. That was years before the major auto manufactures offered them in new cars.

Following the sale of the ranch, brothers Wilson and Dave went to Lovelock to grow potatoes for the war effort and Howard went along with them. While in Lovelock, Howard turned to driving truck for ONC Truck lines hauling freight to and from Reno.

During the late '40s, Howard met Virginia Rose Correll while in Lovelock and

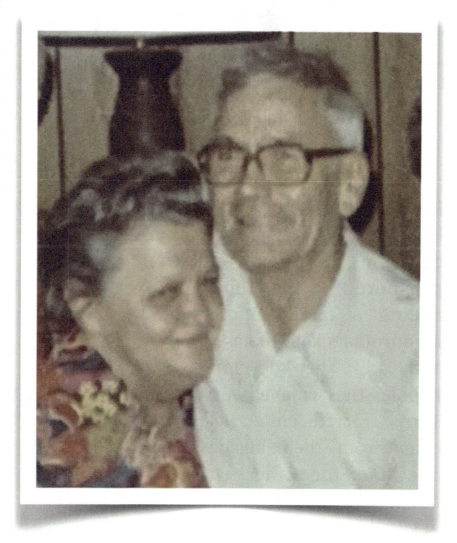

they married on December 7, 1948. A few years following that they moved to Babbitt, Nevada where Howard was employed by the Naval Ammunition Depot. He worked restoring old military ammunition there for a number of years.

Virginia and Howard

While in Hawthorne, Howard and Virginia adopted three children, Henry (Butch), Karl, and sister Diane. This was a brand new exciting experience for all of them but very rewarding. Howard and Virginia loved having children and being involved in all their activities.

In the years that followed, they took the children and moved to Reno and then finally to Fernley where they owned and operated laundromats for an occupation. This proved to be a profitable decision for them and they prospered. They found that raising a family and owning laundromats kept them very busy and, still, they developed two hobbies they enjoyed very much. They started collecting silver coins from their businesses as one and the other was rock hounding. Their spare time was devoted to these two endeavors. Many spare hours were spent in the back country looking for that special stone.

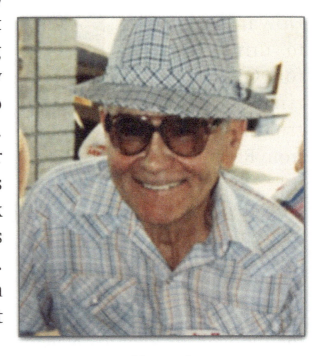
Howard

Butch & Roycella

Howard and Virginia's oldest adopted son was named Henry Slade but they called him Butch. He was born in 1945 and married in 1965 to Roycella Thornburg (1967 - 2006). Butch and Roycella had three children. The first was Nathaniel Slade McGowan (1966 - 1998) who married Sherri and had a son. Butch's second child was Terri Leanne McGowan (b. 1968) who married Orvis Wilmes and had a daughter, Elizabeth Roycella McGowan, in 1987. Elizabeth had one girl and one boy. Terri and Orvis welcomed a second child, a son, LeRoy Wilmes, who was born in 1989. Butch and Rosella's third child, Kimberley Dawn (b. 1970) married a man named Phillips and had two boys, Kile Lewis  Phillips and Christopher Phillips; she later married a man named Hodgson and had one daughter, Kenedee Lynelle Hodgson. Butch died in 1974.

Karl & Janet

The second adopted son of Howard and Virginia, Karl Edgar was born in 1947 and, in 1968, married Janet Schlarman, born in 1947. They had three sons. The first, Bret was born in 1967 and is deceased. Their second son, Brad, was born in 1967 and has one daughter and a son. Their daughter, Misty Ann, was born in 1988. Their son, Karl Ryan, was born in 1990. Karl and Janet's third son,

Howard Joseph, was born in 1972 and married Joy Powers in 1995. They have five girls, Abigail Evelyn born December 12 1996, Brenna Alice born in 1998, Claire Elizabeth born in 2001, Danielle Marie born in 2003, and Emma born September 1, 2007.

Diane & David

Howard and Virginia's third adopted child, Diane Turner McGowan Powers was born in 1949 and married David Lawrence Powers Jr (1946 - 2016) and had two sons and a daughter. The first son, Kevin Eric Powers, married Patricia Ravenscraft and had one son, Curtis Lee Ravenscraft, who has one son and two grandsons. Diane and David's second child, Brian Keith Powers, was born in 1974 and in 1998 married Michelle Hunt Powers, born in 1978, and had three sons and one daughter. Their first son, Jacob Gage, was born in  1997. Jacob has a son and a grandson. The second son of Brian and Michelle, Caleb Ryan, was born in 2002. Their third son, Dylan Thomas, was born in 2005. The daughter of Bryan and Michelle, Kamryn Leigh, was born 2006. Diane's and David's third child, a daughter named Cheryl Rene Powers Chamblee Andrews, was born in 1976 and married Trevor Chamblee (b. 1976) in 1996. They had one daughter named Michaela Diane Chamblee born in 1996. Cheryl was divorced in 2002 and married John Andrews and had a son, Shawn Mathew Andrews, born June 23, 2002 and died September 15, 2002.

13

David T. McGowan Family

The fourth child of John G and Elizabeth J McGowan was yet another boy. He was born on July 14, 1913, and they named him after both of his grandfathers, David and Terrence. He was born at the ranch house in Missouri Flat in the southern corner of Mason Valley. "Dave' was born a very healthy baby and continued to be strong and healthy. He attended the Plummer Country School that was one mile east of the ranch house where he and the family lived. He enjoyed being a young farm boy and all the responsibilities that came with it. He loved animals and was a good hand at attending to their needs. His speciality however, was anything mechanical. From the start, he found mechanical equipment to be what he liked the most about being a farmer. This proved helpful as he grew and had a family of his own to support. He enjoyed working in the shop with his older brothers, Wilson and Howard, and became very proficient at repairing and building things needed on the ranch. All the McGowan boys became quite good at blacksmithing, which saved the ranch considerable expense. Dave and his brothers enjoyed doing most anything that helped. This was the "Roaring Twenties" and all of Mason Valley was busy producing agriculture and ranch products.

Dave went to high school in Yerington at Lyon County High School. He was a good student and was quite popular among the

other students. His older brother, Wilson, drove him and other nearby farms kids to school. Dave was an outstanding football player and voted to the All-State Team.

It was in high school that he met his future wife, Frances Alice Perry. They dated and married a few years later on February 12, 1936 at the McGowan Ranch, which would be their home for a number of years. They lived-in the Little Red House that was across the farmyard from the main farmhouse. Wilson and Marie took over the ranch house while John and Beth, with their teenage daughter, Katherine, moved to a small home they remodeled a quarter of a mile east.

Dave and Frances lost their first child at birth, a boy, George Frank, on February 4, 1936. However a bouncing new boy, David

Wilson McGowan, was born on September 25, 1938; he was greeted with much happiness and joy. Just a little over a year later, on Dec 8, 1939, a daughter arrived and was named DeAnn Frances McGowan. Both of their first children were born at the McGowan ranch. A final son, Curtis Barton McGowan, was born March 24,1946, in the Yerington Hospital. Dave and his family remained for one year to help manage the ranch. It sold in 1946 to Will Rouse.

Dave took his family to Lovelock to raise potatoes for a year with his brother Wilson in Lovelocks' Lower Valley. While they had

Curtis, Frances, David W,
David T & DeAnn

success growing potatoes there, Dave longed to be in Mason Valley so he brought his family back to Yerington the next year. He then purchased an established feed and grain business called The Farmers Mill, located on West Bridge Street, and owned the business until 1953 when he accepted a job at the Anaconda Weed Heights Copper Mine. He worked there as a welder until his medical retirement in 1973. Dave and Frances lived on McGowan Lane, one mile west of Yerington. Frances was a very busy person her whole life. She grew up in the northwestern part of Nevada with two brothers and two sisters on a homestead north of the Black Rock Desert they called, "the home place". Her father, Frank Perry, at a very young age, fought in the Indian Wars of Nevada. He was a fence builder by trade and traveled a lot. Frances' mother, Alice Perry, was from a Mason Valley family by the name of Osborne. Frances' brothers and sisters were all successful business people in western Nevada and the Bay Area. Frances worked at the Golden Rule Store in Yerington for many years while her children were growing up and following

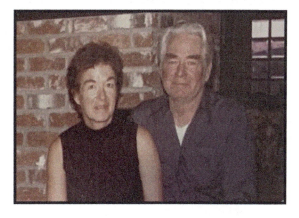

DAVE and FRANCES

that, she took a job as a secretary for the Yerington Intermediate School, where she worked until her retirement.

David & Barbara

David W.McGowan, was born on September 25, 1938 at the McGowan ranch, and as mentioned above, he brought much happiness to the new family. He was a happy child and a pleasure

Daves Signs

to raise. Young David rode the school bus into Yerington to grammar school, where he did very well. Although shy, he made many new friends at school. By the time David entered high school the family had moved to town and David only had to walk a few blocks to school. David's circle of friends grew as did his interests during these years. He had a talent for music and piano which lasted his lifetime.

David W McGowan

Following two years at the University of Nevada, he spent a few years in Oakland, California working for his uncle, Marshall Perry. He then returned to Nevada and began his apprenticeship in sign painting. David married Peggy Mattson and had a daughter Elizabeth D. (b 4/17/62). They divorced in 1964.

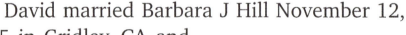

David married Barbara J Hill November 12, 1965 in Gridley, CA and they had 3 children. Barbara worked as a secretary and stenographer in Yerington until her retirement in 2014. David passed away February 19, 2016 in Yerington.

Barbara

David & Barbara

Elizabeth D

David and Peggy's daughter, Elizabeth D. was born April 17, 1962 in Yerington and married Lee Pliscou, a lawyer. They have three children, 2 girls and a boy. They live in Siapan where he does legal work for the country's government.

———————————————

Jennifer

David and Barbara's first child was Jennifer D, born November 13, 1966 in Yerington. She married Kelly Q Carpenter and had 2 boys and 2 girls. She lives in Mountain View, WY. Jennifer is a grocery store manager. Kelly passed away on November 11, 2023, after a bout with brain cancer.

Lynetta

Lynetta R, their second child, was born February 27, 1969 in Yerington. She married Darin. Dearden and they have 3 boys and 2 girls. They live in Fillmore, UT. Darin works for Cox Automotive and Lynetta is a clerical worker.

David T

David T, the third and last child of David and Barbara and was born May 8, 1970 and married Char M and had 7 children. They live in Spanish Fork, Utah where he is employed by Textonic Steel and does detailer work for the company.

David, Barbara, Lynetta, David T & Jennifer

David W McGowan Family 2009

DeAnn & Bob

DeAnn

DeAnn Frances Fabri was born 12/18/1939, in Yerington. She was very active in school her whole life. In high school she participated in editing the yearbook, cheerleading, speech and debate, and student council activities. She then earned her teaching degree from the University of Nevada and taught 37 years in three different schools for Washoe County, Nevada. During this time she earned many awards for her exceptional abilities. DeAnn taught in a parochial school following retirement.

She married Charles (Bud) Mason in Yerington following graduating from the University of Nevada and they had a daughter, Monet, born on October 22, 1966. They divorced in 1969. DeAnn married Robert (Bob) Fabri, from Yerington. Living in Reno, Bob worked for the Nevada Highway Dept., FNB bank appraising, and RMC Construction Loan Co. as an inspector. They had a son, Robert in 1973.

Bob

DeAnn & Bob

DeAnn and Bob owned a cabin at Twin Lakes,CA and later a home at Graeagle, CA. Bob Passed away September 9, 2017 and DeAnn just four months later on Bob's birthday, January 3, 2018.

Monet

Ted

Monet M Mason Fabri, the first child of DeAnn, was born and raised in Reno and graduated from the University of Nevada, is now a Reno school teacher. She married Theodoros (Ted) Paputsidis from Greece in 1992. They had two children, Elena and Mihalis. Mihalis died in 2023. Monet and Ted live and work in Reno.

Ted - Elena - Mihalis - Monet

Ted- Carter- Elena—Monet

Robert

Robert A was born to Bob and DeAnn in Reno and attended school there. He graduated from the University of Nevada and is a self-employed architect who owns FormGrey Studio LLC architectural services in Reno. He married Danielle, also an architect, for Van Woert Bigotti Architects. Robert and Danielle have two boys, Lucas Michael and Nathan Perry.

Danielle, Lucas, Nathan, Robert

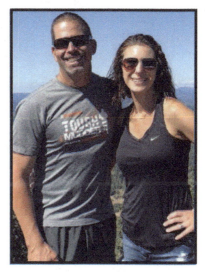

Robert & Danielle

Bob and DeAnn Fabri Family

Curtis and Johnny

The last child of Dave and Francis was Curtis B, born March 24, 1946, in Yerington. He went through the twelfth grade there.

Curtis

Following high school graduation in Yerington, he married Dee Domenici and they had three children; Curtis Jr, Shelly, and Terrance. He learned the auto body repair business and spent the next twenty years working for automobile dealers and himself. Custis and Dee lived in Chico, Reno, Carson City, Yerington, and Fallon.

Curtis and Dee divorced in 1971. He then married Johnneta (Johnny) Craig in 1972. She worked for the county district judge in Fallon, Nevada for the Third District Court. Curtis changed occupation to upholstery making, specializing in outdoor sporting equipment. Johnny passed away December 30, 2014. Curtis lives in Fallon enjoying the outdoors, mostly fishing.

Johnny

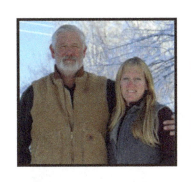
Cirtis & Sara

Curtis B Sr. and Dee's first child Curtis B Jr was born December 3, 1964 in Yerington. He has lived in Fallon since he was eleven and he is a carpenter and custom knife maker of some renown. He married Sara E Camper in 2018 who has a son, Tim W. Camper and is a Special Education teacher for Churchill County School District in Fallon.

Michele & boys

The second child of Curtis and Dee was a daughter they named Michelle 'Shelly", born May 27, 1966, in Carson City. After high school, she went to San Diego State and graduated with a degree in history and a minor in sociology. Michele adopted 3 boys, Alex, James and Aaron and they live in San Diego. CA, where she is a special education advocate.

Kate, Terry & boys

Terrance A 'Terry' was the third child born to Curtis and Dee McGowan, on November 9, 1968. He married Catherine B 'Kate' Manhire, February 10, 1990, and had two boys, Trey A and Conner C McGowan. Terry is a cowboy/rancher and custom saddle maker with worldwide customers. Kate is a mathematics teacher in Fallon. Trey married Sarah Lynn Johnson on September 18, 2019. Conner was tragically killed November 10, 2019.

Curtis Jr, Johnny Shelly, Curtis Sr. & Terrance

14

George S. and Cora McGowan

On February 16, 1915, John G and Elizabeth J McGowan welcomed George Sanford, their fifth child and last boy. George was a very busy and energetic child. He had four older brothers to keep watch on him as he grew up. He went to grade school at Plummer Country School, just one mile west of the ranch house. He was forever getting into mischief at school only to hear from his stern father when he got home. George was the 'apple of his mother's eye' and knew he could get protection from anyone by finding mom.

There was a family story that George caused the buggy to take off just as the schoolteacher was stepping off, causing it to run over her leg as they were arriving at the schoolhouse. George with his usual big smile never admitted to any wrongdoing. While he, like his brothers, was taught how to do farm chores as a young boy, he was also very good at hiding when work was to be done. As he grew into manhood, he became much more reliable when it came to contributing to the farming effort. George went to Lyon County High School in Yerington as a teenager and was a good student. He participated in a number of extracurricular activities along with regular studies.

He was well-known for practical jokes by the family. Most anything could be expected from George. One of his brothers told of a time the new Superintendent of Schools was at the ranch with

his wife for a social visit as dinner guests of John and Lizzie. John was the President of the School Board at the time. Things were progressing well when all of a sudden the front door popped open and in rode George on his favorite horse. "I Just wanted to meet the new Superintendent." said George. John, his father, not a bit pleased, chased him out with a few unkind words. Now George thought that was humorous, but his dad didn't agree.

GEORGE

Following high school graduation George worked on the ranch and helped with the regular work of ranching and farming. He and another local young man, George Hilbin, started a house painting business for the Mason Valley area. The two Georges were quite a pair. They both had a liking for whiskey and tended to party and frolic a good deal. Not a great amount of painting got done, but some. They also did wallpapering when they had time. Life was a lot of fun for the Georges.

The stock market crash of 1929 ushered in the Great Depression. President Hoover and President Roosevelt, taking over in 1933, struggled desperately to turn the economy around. Then the Second World War started in Europe and on December 7, 1941, the Japanese Empire bombed Pearl Harbor and forced Roosevelt to declare war. This was followed by a tremendous number of volunteer enlistments into the military by American men. Among those were cousins, George S and Frank M McGowan, who joined the military effort. They were taken into the Army Air Corp and

GEORGE MCGOWAN
US ARMY AIR CORP

sent to boot camp to become soldiers together. Both were later transferred to the Philippine Islands. They were captured by the Japanese and made to surrender following the Battle of Bataan. After this, they were forced into the famous "Bataan Death March" from Corregidor to the prison camp, O'Donnell, almost 70 miles distant. Over the course of the march, the men were given little food or drink and were subjected to torture by the Japanese. There were between 500-650 American deaths and thousands of Filipino deaths.

The war in the Pacific was a brutal conflict that required the U.S. and its allies to recapture, one by one, each island and territory that the Japanese had originally invaded and taken. By 1944, the U.S. began to win each grudging battle. Slowly the Philippines and Burma were regained,

but each battle came at a brutal cost of human lives. Although some Japanese prisoners were taken, most fought to the bitter end. In Okinawa, when the battle finally ended, the Japanese had lost 94% of their original force.

The war in Europe had progressed well for the U.S. and its allies, and on May 8, 1945, Nazi Germany surrendered. However, the Pacific battle lingered on at a high cost of lives. President Harry S. Truman along with a majority of his generals and advisors decided to end the brutal cost and dropped the first atom Bombs on Hiroshima and Nagasaki on August 6-9, 1945 with an extreme loss of lives. Japan finally surrendered the losing battle August 10, 1945, officially ending WWII.

George and others escaped captivity while in the Japanese prison camp. Harrowing stories were told of swimming across a river while attempting to reach friendly guerrilla forces, only to find the logs they thought were so bothersome to swim around were not logs, but alligators!

George was being rehabilitated at a military hospital in Seattle when he met his future wife, Cora Bell Tandy, a beautician. They married December 4, 1945 in Seattle, Washington. Their marriage did not last very long after they returned to Yerington to live. Bouts of heavy drinking and major disagreements over many issues, along with the terrific Post-Traumatic Stress from the war added to their troubles. They were troubles that would haunt George the rest of his life. The military attempted to rehab George at many facilities for years following his discharge, but nothing seemed to have a lasting effect. He was awarded a Military Pension, but lived a very sad life.

GEORGE & CORA

In the latter part of George's life, he became quite serious about painting, much like his mother, who was a very accomplished artist. He became quite good at portraiture. When he would finish portrait painting, he would get great joy in giving it to the subject.

George's life ended sadly. While on a ride into the Pine Nut Mountains by himself on January 23, 1990, he had car trouble and was found nearby, having died of hypothermia.

15

Katherine and Dean Buchanan Family

The sixth child of John G and Elizabeth J McGowan was the girl they had wanted since their first child was born. It was a very happy occasion to welcome Katherine Louise on June 20, 1922. "Katie" was born at the ranch, seven years after her youngest brother. She became the 'star of the show', being the only girl in a family with five brothers. Both of her Wilson grandparents had already passed away. Her grandmother Louisa Hernleben McGowan was her only living grandparent.

Katie

The president of the United States in 1920 was Warren G Harding and the governor of Nevada was Emmet D Boyle. Our country was beginning to industrialize and Prohibition was instituted.

Katie attended the Plummer Country School about a mile from the ranch house for the first five years of grade school, but finished in Yerington due to consolidation of schools. She attended high school in Yerington and sometimes lived with her brother, Jack and his wife Lou, to avoid traveling. Katie loved to be helpful and as a young girl enjoyed helping her father and brothers on the

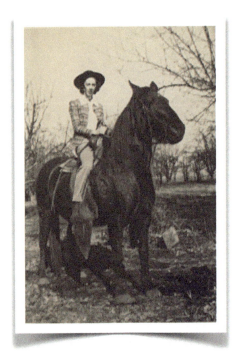

ranch. She liked to drive the tractor, and was called upon to rake hay during the summer. Her favorite past time was riding her horse and helping herd cattle on the Missouri Flat summer range for the ranch.

Following high school, Katie found employment at her Uncle's Mason Valley Bank in Yerington where she worked for a few years. Katie and her girl friend, DD McConnell, whose father was foreman for the Fleischmann Ranch, up the East Walker road about 10 miles from the McGowan Ranch, decided they needed some excitement. Along with two young female schoolteachers seeking jobs, they took a trip to Las Vegas looking for work. The teachers found employment but Katie and DD were not as fortunate, so they headed home. In Tonopah, they decided to apply there and were immediately hired at the Army Air Base a few miles from town. Katie said she was "in charge of counting nuts and bolts" for the airplane repair!

At the Mispah Hotel and Casino she met the man who would become her husband, Dean C (Buck) Buchanan, a young, handsome pilot who was stationed at the Air Base as a pilot instructor. He was teaching young pilots how to fly the B-24 'Liberator' bomber for the Army Air Corp for Uncle Sam. Buck was a seasoned pilot with over 50 bombing missions in the WWII European Theater, with considerable success! The B-24 was the most widely used bomber of WWII. The

B-24 bombing raid

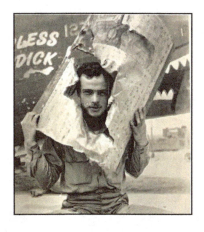

Flak damage to his plane

U.S. manufactured more of these than any other bombers. Katie, as it happened, liked to go into the ballroom of the Mizpah Hotel and Casino and play the piano in the evenings. It was there that romance started, not quickly, but eventually. Katie thought Buck

was "quite brash" to start with. But it wasn't long and they were inseparable. Love was in the air!

During their romance period, Buck flew a 'mission' from the air base in Tonopah to the McGowan

B-24 Liberator bomber

Ranch in Mason Valley, to shake up the locals! Seeing a lone B-24 Bomber making low flying passes at treetop height was quite a spectacular sight for the ranchers of the south end of Mason Valley. It caused quite a stir in Yerington!

It wasn't long after this that the wedding took place at the McGowan Ranch on June 3, 1945. It was quite a celebration with all the "whistles and bells" and relatives from near and far in attendance.

with Beth   Wedding couple   with John

Katie and Buck became very happy parents while they lived in Kansas City, as their first born, Kathy Lou was born 1946 and Christopher three years later on June 27, 1949. The family lived in Kansas until the mid sixties when they moved to Detroit, Bucks new domicile with TWA. It was here that son Donald John was born November 29, 1954.

Wedding top Beth Buck John
Howard bottom Wilson Katie Jack
George Dave

In Michigan, Buck started flying TWA's new Constellation airplanes. They were considered the beauties of the air, as they were fast and could fly long distances to make overseas flights. The Connies, as they were called by the pilots, were the most

Constellation

heavily used planes flying at that time. Buck advanced to the airline's captain position, flying Connies on international flights. He was soon called up to fly the new 707 four engine giant jet. It flew from New York to Cairo, Egypt and points further. This required the family to adjust to the life of an international pilot, with dad being gone a lot of the time. As Buck progressed with TWA, the family found themselves moving to new areas to live. From Detroit they moved in the mid 60's to the west coast and Costa Mesa, California, the land of sunshine and beaches. Having to commute to New York to fly his assigned routes overseas became a necessity for Buck. To compensate for

the drudgery, Katie and Buck joined other TWA pilots families. They bought a condo in Maui, Hawaii to enjoy and relax on both vacations and Buck's long breaks between flights. In the meantime, the kids were growing and going to school. Kathy, the oldest, started college at nearby Orange State College. Chris was in high school and Don in grammar school. Kathy also spent considerable time flying to Germany to visit and spend time with a friend.

KATHY CHRIS & DON

Family members were allowed to fly free to anywhere the company flew. She ultimately graduated Orange State in the early 70's.

The Buchanans moved to South Shore Lake Tahoe. They were

McGowan Women Meeting
top row Kathy McClintock, Kelly Garcia, Kim Miller, Brooke Bernard, Carolyn Bernard, Sallie Bernard, Bottom Katie, Jackie Perkins, Donna Derico, Kris Perkins

finally back in Nevada after many years. They first lived in Round Hill Village and then moved to a home on Kingsbury Grade. They were 'home' and both very happy! The children all married after the family moved to Nevada. Living in Nevada allowed a new opportunity for the Buchanan children to work in the gaming business. Kathy became an excellent "21" dealer for Harveys

Wagon Wheel Saloon at South Shore. Brother Don, as he was old enough, became one of Harveys' top bartenders, a position he held for many years. Brother Chris found adequate employment in the building trades at Lake Tahoe and the surrounding area.

In the late 70's Buck had a stroke which forced him to retire from flying in 1980. He went back to college and attempted numerous other activities, but he found retirement rather difficult. Buck passed away in 1985. Following Buck's death Katie immersed herself in her daughter Kathie's love of politics. Katie joined the Tahoe Republican Women's Association, followed by the Nevada State Republican Women's Association, where she won many awards for her service.

In her later years, Katie relished her role as the matriarch of the McGowan family. She helped host the "Pizen Switch Roundup" which ran for many years for old friends and family members to gather in the Yerington area and enjoy old friendships and reminisce over food and drink. She also gathered the McGowan Women together annually to keep the old family memories alive as years passed. In the early 2000's, Katie moved to Gardnerville

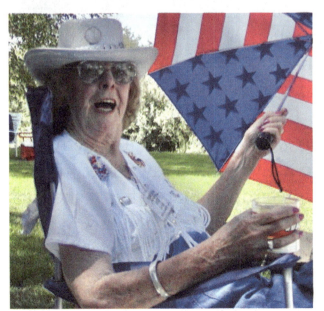

from Tahoe and then eventually to the Kingsbury Grade area to finish her long life. Wherever Katie was, she always found a way to make people happy and spread her "kindness" to many people. She lived to be almost 99 years old, dying April 21, 2021.

Katie's 80th birthday party

Kathy

Kathy

Kathy Lou McClintock, the oldest child of Katie and Buck, was born in Kansas City on August 18, 1946. She lived in Bellville, Michigan, then Costa Mesa where she finished both high school and college. In 1970, when it was time to settle down, Kathy moved to Carson City to be near her Nevada family. Her parents and brothers followed a few years later. She worked for Harvey's Wagon Wheel Casino as a games dealer for 16 years. In the mid 70's, she married Bob McClintock. They divorced a number of years later. In 1991, she moved to Carson City and began a career in furniture sales for Carson/Winan's Furniture. She then entered the insurance business with American Family Insurance until her retirement. She is enjoying her membership in the local Carson City

Bob & Kathy

Kathy

Lions Club with all its work and activities. She is also active with Eddy Street Vintage Market in Gardnerville, where she has been able to use her talent both in sales and creative abilities. Kathy has always been a people person with many friends, especially among family.

148

Chris

Christopher D, born June 27, 1949, has always been an active person. He was especially fortunate during high school to be able to take industrial trade classes of carpentry and woodwork, electrical and electronics, drafting and mechanical, all of which he's utilized over the years. He has enjoyed a life of working with his hands as well as his mind.

Chris

"Chris" spent two years in the U.S. Army after he graduated high school.

He was married to Sheri Wolf in the 70's, who brought a daughter to the marriage named Heather. Cheri and Chris

agreed that marriage was not meant for them and divorced.

In 1975, Chris went to work for his uncle, Howard McGowan, as his handyman in the laundromat business. He later leased and owned the businesses on his own. Chris also helped Howard on his project of refurbishing the Elm Tree Cemetery in Mason Valley by the McGowan ranch, which was built by David Wilson, Howard's grandfather many years before. Following Howard's death, Chris continued the cemetery work in his uncle's honor.

Don & Terry

The last Buchanan child was Donald John, born in Michigan on November 29, 1954. He was a lively little guy from birth.

Harvey's

Don was a good student, busy, and full of mischief.

When the family moved to Nevada, he went to work for Harvey's Wagon Wheel Saloon as a bus boy. When he was old enough he was hired as a bartender and quickly worked his way up to the top, working all the best bars in the casino, including "the Top of the Wheel". After Harveys was bombed by an extortionist in 1980, Don decided to go elsewhere to tend bar. He worked at the Pony Express, the Lakeside, the Carriage House, and others for a few years

Don married Terry L Ludlam, in 1987 and they bought a home in the Gardnerville Ranchos where they continue to live.

The big change in his life came in 1987 when he went to work for Bentley Company in Minden. Bentley later sold to G.E. and Baker Hughes. Don

Don & Terry

worked there 27 years until retirement.

Don's favorite hobby over his lifetime was hunting and fishing. He loved being out in the Nevada countryside and enjoying the wide-open space and freedom. Don passed away March 4, 2024 due to acute liver failure. Terry followed him March 26, 2024 in death.

16

COMING HOME

The Great Depression of the 1930's had a severe effect on the state of Nevada. Mining in most of the state was either closed down or in the process of closing. Large numbers of workers were without jobs. The farming industry was barely surviving with very little demand for its products. Businesses with large operating loans were in perilous positions.

The McGowan Ranch which had grown rather rapidly through the use of bank loans, struggled like many others. Sheep for which they had paid 12 dollars, were now worth three. All the products were only worth a small percentage of their previous value. Owners were scrambling for 'cash' crops to survive. Banks were closing. By changing the ownership of the McGowan Ranch and getting some help from the Federal Land Bank and the National Fraser Lempke Act (which gave farmers three years to settle debt,) the McGowans paid all their debts and survived.

David and Abigail Wilson completed their lives living on the

Missouri Flat Cemetery

McGowan Ranch which they had owned for over 40 years. It was where they started life in Mason Valley in 1863. Abigail died August 17, 1910. David lived a few more years until April 25, 1915. They both are buried at the Missouri Flat Cemetery in Mason Valley, the property for which they had donated.

My grandfather, John, decided one summer day in 1945 it was time to teach first grandson, 'Frank,' to drive. So, off we went in the ole farm pick-up, with eleven year old Frank barely able to see over the hood. Following some humorously jerky starts, learning to operate a clutch and shifting a manual transmission, the shout of, "Watch where you're going!" saved us from clipping a tree. We were finally doing fairly well, going down the highway to grandpa's house. Getting off the highway required a left turn into the yard, followed by a fancy right, then a quick left turn into the parking spot. I remember turning off the highway and stepping on the gas, but froze on the next turn and made a very large u-turn through his giant farm garden. "I'll be damned!" I remember hearing him say, then...he started laughing, and I thought he'd never stop. Only a grandfather could be so kind!

FAMILY GATHERING - 1945 - Edith, Beth, George, Howard, Deann, Buck, Donna, Cora, Dave, Molly, Jackie, Katie, Lou, David, Jack, John, Frankie and Frank

Wilson, Dave, and their father, John G, were working the ranch together in 1944 when they came to the collective decision to sell. It was a difficult one to make as the ranch was the first property owned by David and Abagail Wilson in Mason Valley. Wilson and Marie and family had moved to Lovelock to raise potatoes for the war effort and were doing well. George was safely back in the United States after escaping the Japanese prison camp in the Philippines. John G and Beth were starting to reach the age of retirement. It would prove to be a daunting task and take a few years, but the ranch was finally sold to 'Will' Rouse in 1946, with the agreement that Dave would remain for one year to teach the new owner the ropes. Dave and Will became very good friends during that year.

The decision to sell the McGowan ranch relieved a lot of pent up pressure on all the principals of the ranch. For the first time in a number of years, John and his sons could go about just being farmers and enjoy their families. The War was almost over and everyone was looking to the future. Katie was planning her wedding in June 1945. Everyone seemed to be doing well.

John and Beth had fun picking out a small new house in southwest Reno for them to spend their later years. They dreamed of the times they would spend with family, especially their grandkids. His brother Ted lived in Reno and they were excited they would finally be together. Beth's brother, J I Wilson also was living in Reno, watching over his financial

John and Beth in Reno Home

Ted McGowan

interests. Two of John's sisters lived in Eureka and Arcadia in northern California, and John and Beth had wanted to visit them for years.

After many years of raising a family and hard work on the old ranch in Mason Valley where Beth's folks originally settled, John and Beth, in 1946, moved to Reno to retire following the sale of the ranch. It was a cozy home in the newer part of town where they intended to live out the remainder of their lives.

In May of the following year, while traveling from Wilson and Marie's home in Lovelock, they were involved in an auto accident on a rainy afternoon heading for Yerington for Memorial Day. The accident took Beth's life and ended the beautiful lifetime partnership of the pioneer children. John was alone and would live the remaining 23 years until 1970 without his lovely wife.

COMING HOME
by John G McGowan

When those days come along and I'm lonely and sad
And it seems I just have to be near,
I wander back again ere I go mad,
to the place that I'll always hold dear.

I turn on the lane and out on the field
Where we strolled many times hand in hand,
then I set on that knoll and try to reveal,
The years when it all seemed so grand.

The cattle in the meadow to be turned on the range,
Would be waiting the mountains beconing call
find the little white faces, heed the cowboys so strange.
When they guide them toward home in the fall.

But, now that I'm here near that dear old home,
When the sun seemed to shine every day,
I find there's no comfort in wanting to roam,
So I'm coming back home to stay.

John spent most of his final years living in Lovelock and Carson with Wilson and Marie, except the last few, during which he lived with Howard in Fernley. John and Beth are buried in Missouri Flat Cemetery in the Wilson plot next to her parents David and Abigail.

Made in the USA
Las Vegas, NV
18 April 2024